AF225621

To my incredible wife

Your strength and faith throughout this hardship
has been an inspiration to me. I love you more than
words can express.

Caleb, Reese and Levi

I'm so proud of the people you are becoming. I hope
that the insight you receive from this book will add
to your faith as you grow in your understanding of
God's great love.

Lord, you are my all in all

My strength, my refuge. I will follow you all the days
of my life and will tell of your love and faithfulness
as long as there is breath in my lungs.

First Printing: 2020

ISBN 978-164786913-7

Self Published by Matthew Hammond
PO Box 925
Sherwood, OR, 97140

www.astoryofrevival.com - This website may or may not be live depending upon the timing of your visit and the direction in which God takes this work. Please reach out with any questions by through Instagram using the handle @mrmatthewhammond. I would love to share our story with your church body or small group.

GLAD I ASKED

A STORY OF REVIVAL

MATTHEW HAMMOND

CONTENTS

"ASK YOUR QUESTIONS!"

INTRODUCTION — "ASK YOUR QUESTIONS!"

In the fall of 2018 I began hearing subtle hints from the Lord that I was supposed to write a book about the chaotic experiences in which my wife and I were living. To say that it was a crazy time is the understatement of the decade.

Lauren and I asked a lot of questions during this two year period and God was incredibly patient as I'm sure our questions often sounded like complaints. Looking back, it seems as if God was leading our steps, while we were repeatedly asking "Are we there yet? Why is this road so long? Is there a bathroom around? Can we get something to eat?"

My kids provided a ton of insight into our predicament during the chaos. But the purity of their hearts differed greatly from my own. I just hope my response to their questioning didn't squash a desire to ask questions of God.

Caleb, Reese, and Levi are fantastic kids! Obedient, good natured, intelligent, slightly mischievous and always very curious about their world. Specific examples elude me at the moment but there are times when they ask for something; for the sake of the example let's say it was a cookie. They'll ask and I will say, "Not right now." Five minutes go by and one of them may ask again, "Dad can I have a cookie." In my mind I've already said "No" but apparently that's not what they've heard. I'll look at them, somewhat perplexed, and say "No, you cannot have a cookie right now." Another hour passes and they'll ask again but by this time, my patience is shot.

Because my work is flexible, on a typical day I'll pick them up from school, hit the grocery store, make them a snack, and start cooking dinner before Lauren comes home from her office; so my evenings are relatively full. As I work through the "to do" list of each evening, my mind focuses in on the tasks at hand, while in the background I think through the day and the coming events of the evening and the following morning.

In addition to being busy, the house is full of sound. Food is cooking on the cast iron skillet, the hood over the range is on high, music may be playing in the background and the three of them are running around our tiny home playing games or arguing over a game gone south. So when one of them asks me again for a cookie, interrupting my train of thought and forcing my brain to engage with a question that has already been answered multiple times, you can imagine the result.

I don't explode but I fail on more occasions than not. I get frustrated that they don't seem to grasp that the answer has been "No" consistently, especially if I've explicitly said, "Stop asking that question." And then my heavenly father gives me a glimpse into my shortcoming as a human father.

Never, not once, has God told me to stop asking questions. He's never exhibited frustration over my repetitiveness or disciplined me for interrupting his train of thought. In his perfect love, God has the time, mental capacity and patience for my questions. Even when they play out on repeat.

Now, I'm not approaching God or asking questions of him with contempt. There is an element of respect that I believe God appreciates, even requires of those who would pose questions to him. Proverbs 1:7 says "The fear of the Lord is the beginning of knowledge, but fools despise wisdom and instruction." This passage is not telling us to fear God, but rather to approach him with an element of respect and sincerity.

That being said, with the covering of the blood of Jesus, the Bible shares a mindset that equips us to approach God, "Let us then approach God's throne of grace with confidence, so that we may receive mercy and find grace to help us in our time of need." (Hebrews 4: 16)

So... What are you doing God!?

This was the unanswered question we played on repeat during our ordeal. If it wasn't posed directly, some derivative of it would be offered up. But here's a thought to consider: if God shared the answer to that question every time I asked, there is no way I would have been willing to walk through the challenges he would present. And those challenges have become the best lessons and reminders for my future.

Imagine if God had actually replied with the answer to your question. "Matthew (or your name), you struggle with X. So, to address it, I'm going to position you to go through countless hardships (fill in your own imaginary details here) so that you'll learn what it means to trust me. I'll equip you with dreams and words of knowledge. But I'm going to make you question my presence as you navigate the hardship. And when you think you're experiencing the most challenging time of your life, just wait a few more weeks. You'll learn that you can actually take more. But believe me son, this hardship is for your benefit so don't be afraid of it. And now that you know all that is to come, don't change any of it."

How do you think any of us would respond!? How would you respond to that? There's no way that we'd allow it to go down without attempting to influence the circumstances.

So God isn't always going to provide us with the answer when we ask for it. BUT... when I questioned God, somehow I felt closer to him, more connected with him; and I felt like the questioning endeared me to him.

God's love is poured out in the times of hardship (both yours and mine). He doesn't want to see us suffer but he loves to watch us grow!

I've written this book in a rather unprofessional manner with the hope of presenting our experience like I would a conversation. When I received back the first edit, I threw out the majority of suggested changes because it altered my voice more than it cleaned up the punctuation or grammatical issues. More than anything I wish I could share the story with each of you in person. Sometimes I still can't believe what God has done and what he is continuing to do in our lives. And please know, I tell this story only to give God glory and inspire others (like you) to reach out to him with questions.

When searching for a title of our personal Odyssey the only thing I could come up with was "What the Hell, God?" Because that's literally what I found myself asking. God... WHAT ARE YOU DOING!?

But I like when people make light of the ridiculous social constructs that exist in our culture. Particularly when they're being edgy to prove a point. Asking God "What the Hell!?" added an emphasis to the writing that accurately represented my feelings at the time the events transpired.

At the same time, this story is also about our revival and I knew that it was supposed to reach those in the Christian community whose walk with the Lord has been shrouded by their own religious mindset.

Using something like "Hell" in the title would have immediately turned them off because the word is akin to a swear word... and "nothing with 'Hell' in the title would be worth a read."

So rather than use "Hell" we kicked around the idea of using the word "Cuss."

"What the Cuss God!?" However that one, in a similar vein, seemed a little too disrespectful. It was certainly edgy enough... maybe a little too edgy. But I was concerned that it wouldn't draw in that segment of the Jesus loving community who were in need of a spiritual defibrillator.

I met with my book designer to talk through the story and brainstorm ideas for the cover. As we discussed titles and subtitles, we kept coming back to "What the Hell God?" And then he suggested a subtitle that I knew would be the answer to our dilemma... "Glad I asked."

This book is about the crazy two year period of life circumstances that lead to the radical revival and transformation of a stagnant faith. In that time, God was using the natural to refine my family in the spirit so that we would be refocused on the calling for our lives. During this chaotic time, we asked more questions of God that we ever had before but at the same time, we had never felt closer to Him.

God has a call on your life, a purpose for which you were created. In order to live out that purpose you will undoubtedly have to grow through your own God-pre-planned hardship and level up to where he wants you to be.

If anything, I hope that this story and the lessons I share inspire you to ask questions of our God as your own hardship hits. The questioning will draw you deeper into relationship with him and once on the other side of the difficult season, you, like us, will be able to say "Glad I Asked."

GLAD I ASKED

"PERSISTENT BUGGER"

CHAPTER 1 — "PERSISTENT BUGGER"

"Listen, I don't understand you. Just sit down and shut up. I'll let you know when I want to hear from you. I'll let you know when I need you. In fact, I'll let you know if I even want you around. Until then just stay put and don't interrupt."

I'd like to think a statement like this would only happen in the movies. Could you imagine your mother saying this to you as a child? Or what if your kids (at any age) screamed this out in the middle of your own attempt to love on them? These words have a cutting effect that puts the recipient in their place. They surge with implications: "Rejection!" "Worthless!" "Misunderstood!"

The great irony in my walk with the Lord is that I was unknowingly saying these things to Holy Spirit without saying a single word.

For 15 years, my relationship with God was based on the "hard evidence" and "logic" found in scripture. Never mind that "hard evidence" is rarely part of our journey or the development of our faith. My God, the God of the Bible, had always been a God of logic, as long as I never looked too closely.

At the time, I would have argued that I was looking far more closely than anyone else I knew. I was involved in leading worship every Sunday, I spoke here and there during midweek services, and I also led the occasional Sunday communion discussion.

I shared my testimony when appropriate and was active in Bible studies with non-believers, which turned out to be anyone who didn't align with my view of what it meant to walk with Jesus.

I argued emphatically about the importance of submission and obedience and the active call on every Christian's life to be a disciple who makes disciples of Jesus. The Great Commission was my marching order and if evangelism wasn't on my mind, my mind was in the wrong place.

The scriptures were clear about the systematic conversion process of every believer: hear the word, believe the word, repent of your sins, confess Jesus as Lord, and be baptized in His name. Period. The end.

This was my standard operating procedure. A structured, logical, process oriented operation. Obviously prayer and personal bible study were baked in there but for the most part, I could "tread water" as long as I knew the scriptures and walked out the Great Commission. Ironically, the amount of guilt I carried throughout those 15 years manifested in arguments with many of the people I loved most and it should have been the primary indicator that something was off... But that's a rabbit hole for another book.

I want to bring your attention back to the paragraph that kicked off this chapter. Without realizing it, I was unknowingly telling Holy Spirit that because I did not understand Him (Him/Her/It/They - Does the pronoun really matter? I'll default to what I'm comfortable with and if you're offended, you probably won't make it much deeper into this read... and honestly, you're probably not my target audience.)

...Him, I told Him to stand in the corner during worship, during prayer, during my personal Bible study, during my teaching Bible studies. It wasn't a spoken directive. It was more of an unspoken non-invitation. I could never understand the practical, current day purpose of Holy Spirit so I never felt the need to invite Him into my daily routine.

> **I could never understand the practical, current day purpose of Holy Spirit so I never felt the need to invite Him into my daily routine.**

During that 15 year period you can imagine what happened:

My worship fell flat - only punctuated by the emotional swings of an upbeat song.

My prayers were unknowingly shallow and I questioned their effect - maybe if I religiously repeated them they would have some kind of impact, but I despised the notion of a monotonously repeated prayer.

My personal Bible study was anemic due mostly to my arrogance - I believed that I knew enough, certainly all that was needed to fulfill the Great Commission; and therefore didn't need to go any deeper. I craved deeper teachings but resigned myself to locking in on those scriptures that would help convert people to Jesus. While those studies produced some fruit and a few people decided to follow the Lord, many studies lacked a significant transformational power that brought the easy burden and light yoke — the one Jesus references. Instead, those studies usually brought with them a yoke of guilt centered around each individual's addictive behavior(s).

That said, you couldn't accuse me of being a Pharisee... I was showing people the scriptures and helping them see the truth. What I failed to grasp was that conveying this truth without first revealing the depth of God's love was leading them to conform to a list of actions, a "to do" or "don't do" list, not unlike that of the Pharisees.

More personally, I felt burdened by the impossible task of living up to my 'potential' — how many Christians could I convert in the next month, year, decade?

I even had a discussion with a close friend about the validity of someone's salvation if they were a "10 Talent" Christian who, in their entire life, only helped one person become a disciple of Jesus; was there any way that "10 Talent" believer would ever measure up to the call of Jesus or the talents they had been given? Would their salvation even be valid?

Even as I write this, it's laughable how pharisaical and monotonous life was without Holy Spirit. I was dry bones teaching others to become dry bones. (Ezekiel 37) Now in fairness, my heart was in the right place — I loved the Lord and I am very grateful for His patience and grace! Despite my lack of understanding, he still moved powerfully in that 15-year period, but nowhere near as powerfully as the years that would follow.

We left our church of 15 years in 2016 after disagreements about the financial setup of the local congregation, as well as the Leadership's stance on what became an epidemic of divorce and remarriage. (Marriages without an invitation to Holy Spirit were failing. Weird, right!?) Our journey took us to a farm south of Portland where we started a house church after being inspired by Francis Chan's movement "We Are Church." Around that time, I believe Holy Spirit began to disregard my restraining order, sneaking around my life when I wasn't looking.

We had always dreamed of raising our kids on land. We first saw the farm on Zillow on a Saturday and toured it the next day with our agent. As we stepped through the front door that Sunday, I immediately felt/heard/ thought (it was unclear at the time which) that we could do a home group there. Somehow Holy Spirit had beaten us to the location to greet and inspire us as we walked through the door. It seemed a bit sneaky, but my wife and I were super excited! By Monday (the next day) we were under contract.

Two weeks later, an acquaintance I hadn't spoken with for two years called to catch up. I told Richard, now a great friend, we were buying a farm and starting a house church. He felt called away from his church and had a deep desire to host a house church as well. A month later, we launched our first gathering together. That, too, seemed a little overly coincidental, like Holy Spirit was weaving his way into our lives to orchestrate our steps.

Over the ensuing 18 months, we had a blast hosting any and everyone who would make their way to Newberg. We had fantastic meals, worshiped with our iTunes playlist, and read through the entire Bible together. We even baptized one of my very best friends in the creek that ran through our farm. We were seeing God move in powerful ways. It was an inspiring time!

Some of the people who joined our group came from a varied Christian upbringing and it made me extremely uncomfortable. But no one ever said or did anything that contradicted scripture, so there was nothing I could readily argue or debate. And at this point we were trying our best to let Holy Spirit lead. But one woman in particular carried an elegant and intimidating grace and her conversations seemed to emphasize Holy Spirit more than anyone I had ever met. Again, this was difficult for me to swallow and she intimidated the crap out of me. (Sorry, ear muffs!) I knew there was no way I could ever fully understand THE Holy Spirit, so I never invited Holy Spirit to hang out. But ever so subtly, my curiosity was aroused, and I began to acknowledge Him a bit more.

Our time on the farm came to an end prematurely after my fear of financial stress and the required commutes for our careers made it clear we needed a shift.

Now, I should tell you that I've only made a few vows to the Lord in my lifetime and two of those vows were:

    1. I will never again live in Beaverton, OR.

    2. I will never again join or be associated with a corporate church.

So naturally, the Spirit picked us up, moved us to Beaverton, and introduced us to a new church body.

The Beaverton explanation is a pretty easy one: I was raised in the country and couldn't stand living in a densely populated suburban community. We had lived in an apartment there once before and it was chaotic. My wife Lauren, however, worked in Beaverton and we found an inexpensive home five minutes from her work - a drastic improvement from her previous two-hour daily commute and a significant monthly savings on our budget. So back to Beaverton we went.

Joining a church is a bit harder to explain, but I'll do my best to simplify: We loved everything about our house church. We loved hosting, we loved the meals, the depth of friendships, the intimacy of worship, the revelations from our Bible studies, everything. It was all good! I never would have guessed that three to four hours of "church" each weekend could have been so enjoyable! It was more like a party than an obligatory meeting. Throughout that 18 month period, I looked forward to Saturday nights (summer/fall) or Sunday mornings (winter/ spring) every week, but after our move we no longer had a suitable location to host.

In addition, my friend Richard felt the Spirit leading him to launch a home church in his neighborhood. Yes, timing played into it, but we also felt God pulling us in a different direction. It didn't feel sneaky at the time but looking back, I smirk as I realize what was going down.

The same year we were hosting church on our farm, I became fast friends with Ben Rose, a fun-loving, fellow goober and work colleague who also happened to be a pastor and co-founder of a small church not far from Beaverton. He had previously invited me to their fellowship, but it never made a ton of sense to go while we were in our groove on the farm. As that dynamic shifted, we had developed some flexibility and could now dip our "weekend worship toes" into the water of whatever Jesus pool we wanted.

Were we church shopping? I hate that term, I'm a buyer not a shopper; never had patience for shopping. But we no longer had a home church either.

To be honest, our first experience at Ben's church was a bit overwhelming.

The severity of the Holy Spirit restraining order had lessened, but we were still far from what we would now call "Spirit Filled." Two things quickly became apparent to us:

1. **This was a hand raising, emotionally charged, Jesus loving group.**
2. **I really wanted to worship that intensely, but I didn't have any clue how to start.**

It was a great overall first impression, but it took a month or two to figure out that we had arrived where Holy Spirit had intended. Weeks later, Ben was preaching on a Sunday morning Christmas Eve service. Without warning, I heard in my soul:

"I want you to teach here."

This was not a point Ben had preached. I don't even remember what exactly he was preaching on. Something spoke directly to me and there was no arguing with it. I felt it deep and knew instantly that this was to become our place of worship; that one day I would be teaching here.

It was a powerful experience, but it gets better. Ben finished his message, the worship team led us through the final song and we began packing up. Quite boldly a stranger, now a good friend, walked up to us and introduced himself. He said, "Hi, my name is Sam and I'm with the teaching ministry here. The Holy Spirit just told me to tell you that you (pointing to me) are supposed to be teaching here and that you (looking at Lauren) are a fire breather."

HOLD THE PHONE! WHAT DID YOU JUST SAY!? WHAT DOES THAT EVEN MEAN!?

Nothing like this had ever happened to us before. Anyone in a church can randomly walk up to a visitor and speak a prophetic word like Sam had, but this was a confirmation of what Holy Spirit had just spoken to me!

It was incredible! The Spirit spoke to each of our hearts and then almost immediately had someone confirm it for us. (After church Lauren told me she had felt drawn to investing in the ministry earlier that morning as well!) We didn't know what we were getting in to, but we knew that at least some of our preconceived ideas about Holy Spirit may have been a bit misguided.

This occurrence kicked off a series of interrelated dreams and life altering events that have become the basis for the following chapters. If you've stuck with me this far, I hope that what follows will have an impact on your walk with the Lord (all of the Lord, Holy Spirit included).

Based on how deliberate Holy Spirit has been in our story, I am certain he is moving in your life as well. In fact, whether you really want it or not, God, through Holy Spirit, is speaking to you, preparing you, and positioning you for a deeper encounter, a resuscitation, a revival.

Regardless of where you stand now, I believe God's passion is to romance your heart and as you will see, whether sneaky or direct, he is relentless in his pursuit.

"FEAR IS A LIAR!"

CHAPTER 2 — "FEAR IS A LIAR!"

Lauren and I were entrenched into a new and very different community after we made the decision to join this crazy Jesus church. Every Sunday I found myself connecting deeper and deeper with the Lord in worship and I could feel Holy Spirit rejoicing each time I poured myself out to Him.

It started one Sunday with burning eyes, a clenched jaw, and a fist gently beating on my chest as the music blasted through the room. I fought the waves of emotion rolling through me as I worshiped the Lord in this new setting. It evolved weeks later into flowing tears, open palms, and a tightening of my vocal cords as I tried to sing. Eventually, the first chord of a familiar song would initiate a strong reminder of His love - tears flowed and I couldn't help but raise my hands in praise. It was worship with abandon, a release of dignity. People faded out as I stood, worshiping my face off before my God. I was in the process of rediscovering the depth of His love all over again but this time with a deeper appreciation of His grace as I evaluated both my pre-Jesus walk and my post-conversion Jesus obedience. His love was and is SO good!

The call to teach weighed heavily on my heart and I strained to figure out where, how and when. There were classes that were held for "new believers" that I attended and soon thereafter began leading but the remaining crustiness of a pharisaical past still frustrated my experience and caused me to raise objections with some of the very basic positions held by this church. I had 15 years of biblical study under my belt and was very familiar with the Christian conversion process but I was beginning to see things through a different lens; one that didn't exactly align with the structure I had been previously taught.

That said, I still couldn't explain the Holy Spirit's call or argue the prophetic confirmation we had received that Christmas Eve morning; so I submitted. "Do what you're gonna do Lord... I mean Holy Spirit... I mean... whoever, just do your thing."

During one of those first classes I attended at the church, I, along with the others there was invited to create mental space to listen to what the Spirit would say to each of us (respectively). At the time, it honestly seemed a little hocus pocus.

I was taught very early on that "the heart is deceitful above all things and beyond cure" (Jeremiah 17: 9) so how could I trust my thoughts or feelings. The only thing I could trust was scripture. Holy Spirit wouldn't speak to me like that, would he? Again, in surrender, I went with it. Besides, I did believe Holy Spirit was living inside me, so why wouldn't He speak?

The specific question people posed that evening was "What do you hear Father God saying to you?"

"Good grief... are we serious? We're just going to put Jesus on the spot like this?" Despite my ongoing skepticism I went with it. After rolling my eyes and clearing my mind I asked the question in prayer and decided to write down the first thing I "heard."

Okay — Empty the thoughts. Imagine myself in my Father's presence and ask the question, "God, what do you see when you look at me?" Even as I write this now, I get a little choked up.

"Matthew, you are a scared little boy, afraid to trust his Father."

I was indignant. "What the heck does that mean!?" I stared at the paper. I looked around to see if anyone saw what I wrote. Then I argued back. "Lord, I'm not afraid to trust you! Is that NOT what I've been doing my entire life? How can you say that!?"

We know that only 10% of communication is verbal, so the vast majority of all communication is defined by the remaining 90%. Intonation, physical presence, mannerisms, voice fluctuation, the emphasis of syllables — they all combine to create meaning behind the words, spoken or written. The beauty of what my Father had said to me that evening was the lack of condemnation within the critique. There was no disappointment or frustration. It was whispered in love, as if God could empathize with my position but wanted so badly for me to walk in something greater.

If I'm honest with myself (and you), it caused a lot of confusion. After processing for a few days I realized there was work to be done. I wanted to trust him and walk out my faith in new ways. But what had been holding me back?

During the fellowship over the ensuing weeks, I caught wind that a group of people had begun a group fast. Individually and as a whole, they were asking God for clarity, wisdom, and a better understanding of what He was doing in their lives. During this fasting period I regularly heard people say "I hear the Lord saying…" or "I felt the Spirit tell me…"

It was a new level of "weird" and my logic loving brain objected. But again, I decided to overrule the objections on the basis of the confirmation we had received a month or two prior. So without invitation, I joined the fast.

"Okay Lord, I want to hear from you too; but I don't want to have to decipher between my thoughts and your voice. So God if you're really speaking, give me dreams."

To accompany the prayer, I decided to start with something easy. Seven days. "God, I'll go seven days on only water."

Ha! "Easy" HAHA!

For those of you unfamiliar with fasting, seven days is the worst possible length to fast (in my opinion) because it's at day seven or eight that your body kicks into a new gear and you actually start feeling much better than the first six. At any rate, I made it four before crumbling under the heavy burden of a Chipotle burrito. Despite breaking and carrying a bit of guilt, I quietly hoped the Lord would still hear my heart and respond. All I can say is God's grace is enough! I had asked for Him to speak through dreams and would be ready for whatever came. He didn't disappoint.

My first dream kicked off in the midst of a group of people who had decided to do something great for the Lord. There was no specific goal. We had simply agreed to get to work on a big project and as soon as we began, someone from within the group began voicing some serious doubts.

"Hey guys, I'm not sure this is possible."

The more he voiced his concerns and subtly objected, the more I felt the zeal and Holy Spirit fire diminishing in the group. The concern progressed into doubt and quickly changed into forms of ridicule for thinking that our goal was even possible. As the man continued, I became aware that whoever this unrecognizable person was, they were filled with a demonic force!

Although I had never experienced anything like it, I decided right then that I would cast this thing out. Uncertain of what to say, I stared at him for a long moment until his gaze, now somewhat maniacal, fell upon me. The lights in the room went dark and suddenly it was just me and him.

"In the name of Jesus, whom I know, I command you to come out!"

That simple phrase doesn't do justice to the events that unfolded. My voice transformed the further I got through the declaration. It seemed to drop to a powerful octave or two below my normal voice and a tangible power echoed from my mouth as I progressed. The further I got through the sentence, the less comfortable the man became. He quickly began convulsing and foaming at the mouth, eyes rolling back into his sockets.

When I concluded the statement a shock wave blasted from my mouth in the general direction of the man and the demon within him screamed in a hoarse, evil roar as he was vanquished. Once the phrase was completed and the demon gone, my eyes shot open and I could feel my heartbeat pounding wildly through my body.

I laid there in the stillness, running the events through my mind in a mild state of confusion. "What the heck was that!? Was that really a demon? Demons don't look like that, do they? How did I do that!?" I knew God had answered my request and I immediately began wondering what Holy Spirit was trying to convey. This dream was violent and quick and wasn't followed by any immediate interpretation. What was the point?

As I consider the years leading up to these dreams and the two since they began, it's become apparent to me that Holy Spirit plays the long game. In as much as we focus on managing the day to day ups and downs, our Father is focused on managing the ups and downs of our lifetime. He is able to disengage from the immediate and consider the expanse of our days, not simply the emotional swings that come with our being fatigued, offended, uncomfortable, etc.

Obviously, God wants us to be righteous in our day to day interactions with him and others. But God's timeline for our perfection is not an immediate switch upon our conversion. For those of you who are going to take the stance of a literal and immediate 180 degree repentance, I've been there. I know the logic behind your stance. I would agree with an element of that line of thinking as it pertains to blatant sin. But riddle me this: When do you "arrive" as a Christian? And Will God ever be finished perfecting you while you remain in this life? Are there not ongoing imperfections within your character to this day that he yet wants to refine?

I don't pose these questions to make an excuse for immediate repentance from the blatant sin. But that's just it... not all of our sin is so obvious. That realization began to shake my 15-year stance of dogmatic rigidity. Soon after this dream, I realized that there will never be a period of time where I can take a "breather" from repenting. I will never earn a "Repentance Badge" for my Boy Scout uniform.

Repentance will forever be a wash, rinse, and repeat process of evaluation, comparison of life to the scriptures, and adjustment. For this reason, I can only encourage people around me to continue in their pursuit of Jesus and the repentance process. Setting expectations of complete and immediate repentance from all sin for those around me is unreasonable and smells suspiciously of the haughtiness God detests.

Unfortunately, a lifetime of poor decisions and agreements with unseen powers had manifested in vices that prevented me from understating true intimacy with the Father.

Now, I don't mean powers in some mystical "universe" explanation. I mean to reference the dark and (typically) unseen spiritual powers; that is to say, demons exist and we can embolden and empower them through the decisions we make. They're the ones who suggest crazy thoughts and ideas that we can choose to grab hold of or ignore. For example, a lustful image popping into my mind - one that had not been anywhere remotely near my train of thought. If I choose to grab hold of this suggestive thought and dwell on it, I figuratively shake hands with the demonic force of lust and that demonic force learns my defensive weak points. Alternatively, if I reprimand that thought, take it captive and throw it out, the demonic presence that suggested it retains no power over my life.

In hindsight, I believe my first dream was a prophetic word from the Spirit showing me what would be happening in the coming season. There would be a need for deliverance from a demonic force in my life and ultimately it would be jettisoned from my spirit through a rather quick but violent process.

God's desire for us is to be perfected into the image of Jesus. It's all about Jesus. And Holy Spirit dwells within us to aid and guide us in the perfecting process.

While I didn't know it at the time, I needed to jettison a number of demonic forces that were preventing me from understanding and growing in His love. But the transformation wasn't going to happen on its own. As the Father had so gently shared, I was a scared little boy, afraid to trust Him. The exorcism process I had seen in my dream was going to take some time despite my nature to want to rush through it.

I know it's a bit early in this read but please allow me to repeat this once more in a way that will make it a bit more personal: You may be unaware of demonic forces preventing you from understanding and growing in His love.

What interrupts your intimacy with the Father? Is it anxiety? Insecurity? Maybe depression? A work schedule? A relationship? Fear?

Can you remember your last intimate encounter with the Lord? Or how to get back there?

The enemy plays with our emotions and likes to make a home in the recesses of our spirit, the places we don't regularly clean out.

In my case, even when fear did unabashedly show up, I was usually so paralyzed by its power that I didn't stop to think through the illegitimacy of its suggestions. Nor was I capable of finding where fear disappeared to when

I came back to my senses. It's elusive — it only came out when it knew that I wouldn't be capable of fighting back or tracking it on my own.

By any means possible, demons wage war against your mind, spirit, soul, and body to interrupt your intimate connection with the Father. If that connection is severed, it becomes easy to forget who we are. And once we lose sight of that identity, who we're created to be, we forget the immense power that flows through us via Holy Spirit.

So here's the truth of the matter, the truth of your power in Jesus:

As a follower of Jesus, you carry a super-natural ability to obliterate strongholds (fear, lust, depression, anxiety, etc.) and to liberate others around you who are oppressed by those powers. You get to inspire them with the overwhelming love of the Father!

Read that again and let it sink in.

It starts with intimacy. If we don't have intimacy with the Father and understand our identity in Christ, what power can possibly accompany our faith? We certainly don't carry a supernatural power on our own!

When God was finished in his creation process, he looked at everything He had created and called it good. When he finished creating man on the sixth day, he declared we were/are very good.

Do you believe he's referring to you when he says that?

No, seriously. Stop and think... do you really believe it? You are God's VERY good creation. You've been crafted in His image, and He is very pleased with you. You are loved by a perfect father who wants desperately to have an intimate relationship with you and his fatherly nature brings with it an adoption into his royal line.

Through the perfect sacrifice in Jesus, your faith brings you into a standing of royalty within His kingdom. That role carries with it the indwelling and outpouring of Holy Spirit's power!

As I stepped deeper into a dynamic intimacy with Holy Spirit, I began to understand my role as a son of the King. But while I could wrap my head around it, I didn't completely buy into it right away. I held back in uncertainty (and fear) of what would happen if I released control… a great example of the power of fear exerting its influence and my inability to root out its illogical suggestions.

For example, raising my hands in worship had never been a culturally acceptable practice for me. So, what would happen if I raised my hands? What would my wife think? What would my friends think?

Bahahahahahaaaa!

Who cares! I know my Father in Heaven was thrilled when I first did it!

If you have kids, think about how awesome it is to watch them dance around the living room and sing or play music or both? Or better yet, how do you feel watching them celebrate when they score in their respective sport! In those examples I believe we get a sliver of understanding of the pleasure God gets out of our unabashed worship.

It took longer than I would have liked but I eventually began seeing how Holy Spirit was wooing my heart. As I released control of my dignity in worship and allowed his love to wash over me, I began envisioning a rough sketch of who He created me to be. There was a blueprint He had drafted and a set of plans for the build. But there was still a lot of work to be done.

You have a blueprint and plans as well, but I promise you this: **you aren't the best builder you know.** Neither am I. We screw things up when we take control of His building process. If we don't get in the way, Holy Spirit will hone us into a masterpiece temple where God's spirit can powerfully reside! That said, He'll never argue with us when we decide to step in and take over in the middle of the building process. Nor will he chastise us when we're ready to admit our need for him to resume building. Our submission is a choice.

"But if service to the Lord seems undesirable to you, then choose for yourselves this day whom you will serve... But as for me and my house, we will serve the Lord." (Joshua 24:15)

I don't think I've ever experienced this while reading a book, but I'm going to pray for you as you read:

Father God, in the name of Jesus I decree a supernatural anointing on every person reading these words. May their eyes be opened to your love and the reality of their standing before you.

God, please provide opportunities to reach a deeper level of intimacy with you, a level of intimacy that is unhindered by the attacks of the enemy. I decree a more complete understanding of their Jesus identity as a result of deeper intimacy with you. I cast out any demonic forces associated with fear, anxiety, sadness or depression that cause hesitation in going deeper with you Lord. Father, as their intimacy deepens and their identity becomes clear, lavish them with gifts of authority!

Holy Spirit, embolden your people with a supernatural power that will result in your glory! May your love overflow through the work of your Spirit within them. I decree supernatural protection from attacks of the enemy over their life and that of their family and friends. Holy Spirit, reveal yourself in a way that would be only from you so their faith would grow in boldness.

Father, you are so, so good! You are worthy of our praise!

Glorify your name!

"EFFECTS OF IDOLATRY"

CHAPTER 3 — "EFFECTS OF IDOLATRY"

"SHE'S CHEATING ON ME!?"

The thoughts raced frantically through my mind and each new line of thinking ripped at my gut. As I processed the series of events that had just unfolded, I realized the love of my life was no longer mine. There are no words to accurately describe my feelings when that realization hit.

In 2018 my wife and I found ourselves walking down the fairway at a local country club on a picture-perfect day. You could say we were experiencing an absence of weather - not too hot and not too cold. The sun was high the afternoon sky and giant cotton candy-esque clouds hovered in stark contrast to their deep blue backdrop. The deep green fairway was lined with 150 ft old growth Douglas Fir trees that created a natural, but forgiving boundary line down each hole. It was beautiful!

I don't recall exactly how we were shooting that day but Lauren is a casual golfer and prefers not to keep score, especially on a date. We had been paired up with a couple of middle-aged dudes that were great for conversation and kept the mood light when one, or most, of our tee shots veered left or right into the line of trees.

After teeing off on the 4th hole we were making our way down the fairway when a random guy in golf attire walked onto the course and approached my wife. I didn't recognize him but I figured they must have known each other from her work at a major sports apparel company just outside of Portland. Seeing someone on the course from the golf division wouldn't be surprising and the two of them struck up a quick conversation en route to our second shot.

I decided to play it cool and keep chatting with the other half of our group while she and this guy wrapped up their conversation before moving down the fairway. Only, they didn't wrap it up. Apparently the guy, I later learned his name was Paul, felt the conversation needed to continue and was comfortable enough that he walked with Lauren as we all continued on towards the green. His presence at that point began bothering me — he was interrupting our date. That being said, I didn't want to be the overprotective, oversensitive, overbearing, and over-whatever husband that would butt into the conversation; so I played it cool as we tapped in our putts and made our way to the next tee box.

To my continued surprise, the conversation didn't end there. He continued walking with us, talking with Lauren, MY Lauren, as myself and the other two guys in our foursome teed off. To make it worse, I had to interrupt their conversation to let her know that it was her turn to tee off.

She seemed startled by the interruption and hurried to the ladies tee box to take her swing... which she crushed! In fact, she almost hit it past one of the other gentlemen's tee shot. For someone who rarely hits the ball, it was amazing! We all stood there clapping, including Paul, whose emotional intelligence must have been in the negatives. How could he not be aware that his presence was interrupting a round of golf, a date, a conversation, and a glorious day? Lauren smiled humbly after watching her ball sail straight down the fairway and returned her club to her bag.

Rather than close things out with the guy, they re-engaged their conversation. This time I brought it up with the other two in our foursome and made some light comments, "What d'you suppose is this guy's deal?" They agreed it was a bit odd and I was reassured that at least my assessment had been accurate.

By the time we got to Lauren's ball, I was past the point of being incredulous. The two of them had been walking 10-15 feet behind the rest of us and while I couldn't hear what they were discussing, I could hear them laughing and both engaging actively in the conversation.

For a bit of context, Lauren and I were married in 2005. I tried wooing her once in the summer of 2003 but she wanted nothing to do with me after our first date. Apparently, she felt like she was being interviewed but I just wanted to get to know her. It was doomed from the start.

But six months later she asked me out. Rather than try and play it safe I made my intentions very clear by stating (somewhat naively) "I can't be friends with attractive women."

It was true. I was either attracted to someone (very much so in Lauren's case) or I wasn't, but I certainly wasn't going to be friends with someone in whom I had interest if we could be dating and discovering if we meshed well together on a grander scale. Nor was I going to be friends with an attractive woman once I had committed to a girlfriend/fiance/spouse. Despite my ridiculous statement on that second date, Lauren stuck around. We formalized our dating relationship in April of 2004, announced our engagement 9 months later, and said our vows in June of 2005. At the time of this writing, we have three incredible children (born in 2009, 2013, and 2017) and have gone on some pretty fantastic adventures together. In all that time, we've never hit a bumpy section that commonly interrupts the honeymoon stage of marriage. We've certainly had our share of disagreements and difficulty, but we have always had the mindset that our marriage is a sanctuary. We love it. We work hard to protect it and we hold no secrets.

With all that in mind, you can imagine my dismay during our time on the course. I was hurt. I still hadn't reached the point of being the dominant husband who would interrupt the conversation and ask the guy to politely 'take a hike' but I was certainly playing out that scenario in my mind and maybe I should have. My hope was that this next shot would give me a window to make a connection with the guy and subtly inform him of his impudence. But Lauren didn't realize that we were at her ball. I looked at the other two guys as we waited patiently for her to address the ball. When it was apparent she had no idea it was her shot I chimed in, "Your shot babe."

No apology, no embarrassment. Just a quick, "Oh hey, would you pick it up for me? I'll come back in at the next hole."

"I'm sorry... what? Are you serious!?"

I was pissed and it was clear the other two guys were uncomfortable. It was also clear that neither this intruder nor my date were aware of the effect their little detour was having on our collective afternoon. Stewing in my juices, I begrudgingly finished the hole with the other guys and we headed to the next tee box. If you figure on a 10-15 minute completion per hole (we're not that great at golf), the two of them had been talking intently for at least a half-hour.

We got to the next tee and all three guys hit from the white tees and again politely waited for Lauren to pause her conversation, in which she was now completely enamored. Only, she didn't get the memo. Again, I had to interrupt the conversation and remind her that it was her shot. However, this time she replied she was going to sit this one out as well and went back to her conversation.

"Nope! Not okay! Not going to continue! This is our date. We're now making the other pair in our group uncomfortable. This is done." I thought, and I made my move. As I approached, I finally made eye contact with the guy and then looked at my wife.

Now, maybe you can remember that time in high school when you just started dating someone new. If that's the case, then you probably also remember the burning feeling in the pit of your stomach every time you saw that special someone in the halls. You know what I'm talking about, that stupid infatuation that made your teenage brain go crazy with all those endorphins and crap. Well, little did we know back then that the infatuation is easily spotted by grounded, emotionally stable adults.

Oddly enough, as I approached my wife and this stranger, I sensed that dynamic electricity, that teenage infatuation. They were almost startled when I abruptly interrupted their conversation. "Excuse me..."

As I spoke the words, the sentence trailed off and a forming emotional tsunami sucked all the emotional water in my ocean out to sea. My brain struggled to process all that I was now taking in.

My wife was developing - no - already had feelings for this guy. Wait, she had touched his arm and was leaning in toward him while they laughed at a private joke. They didn't just know each other, they knew each other.

My mind spiraled. Were they? No. No way! They couldn't be... Could they? How could they be this brazen about it, interrupting our date and carrying on while I was present?

I had never been in shock before but I immediately lost all sensation in my body. As I processed through the wave of emotion that was now slamming into me, I felt an incredible jealousy welling up in my soul.

This guy, this ugly dork with the giant gap in his top front teeth, this schmuck (Is that a swear word? I don't think I would have cared in that moment but I'm sorry if that surprises or offends you) had my wife totally enamored and had already pulled her heart away from me.

Somehow I knew they had already been intimately and emotionally connected.

I felt anger! No, I felt rage that my partner had been stolen from me right under my nose without the least bit of concern or hesitation about how I may object. I felt foolish for not seeing it earlier or interrupting it before lines were crossed. I felt a deep pain — imagining my wife in the throes of passion with someone else. I kept seeing the intimate details of their affair, a vision that I couldn't rip from my mind.

Then came the most surprising and debilitating emotion of all, helplessness. There was absolutely nothing I could do to interrupt this connection without hurting her in the process. I was broken, desperate. I ached all over.

And then I woke up. I sat in the dark of our room, listening to the pounding rain on our bedroom windows along with my own rapid breathing. My head was drenched with sweat and the emotions of the dream still felt raw and VERY real.

In the dream, my wife had been intimately and passionately involved with another man and I was experiencing every bit of the emotional trauma that accompanied such an event. I turned and glanced at my bride, my partner, the woman who held my heart and tried to reassure myself it was just a dream. I even laid down next to her and wrapped my arms around her just to convince myself that she was there in our bed, and not in another. I pleaded with the Lord to take the thoughts away but they persisted so I pulled a journal from my nightstand to jot down the dream.

It took me about 15 minutes to write everything out and as I replayed the scenario in my mind I heard a gentle whisper speak a message that rocked me to my core...

"This is how I feel when you stray."

It was like a concussion grenade went off in my mind. The realization slammed me all over again. All the pain, jealousy, anger, & helplessness.
"God, you feel all this!?"

We all know that marriage can be used as a tremendous metaphor for many fantastic life lessons, but I won't head that direction now because the story didn't end there. God, Holy Spirit, Jesus, they had all shed light on the raw emotion produced by my (and our) adultery and it was in this wave of emotions that I became convinced the Lord had revealed to me these emotions so I might be able to convey them as a teacher myself.

There are an incalculable number of idols in our world today - far more than what Paul encountered in Greece (Acts 17). Social media itself is neutral in this regard but it has become a great example of modern-day idolatry. Every day, we create miniature altars of and for ourselves! We post pictures, statements, and videos in the digital space to acquire social media's currency of engagement - to be 'followed', to be 'liked' - some in the hopes of acquiring monetary wealth, others in the hopes of validation.
While that doesn't apply to all social media usage, you get the idea. And that's a relatively simple example of idolatry... a sin easily identified and easily resolved. When we start talking about the idolatry and ideology of politics (progressives vs. conservatives) or secularism and the pursuit of pleasure, we get to a much deeper level of idol worship. Prestige and pleasure are two very powerful principalities that have been around for many thousands of years and are woven into the fabric of our every day lives. In all seriousness, as followers of Jesus, we can easily be pulled into this idolatry all the while knowing nothing of our sacrilege.

I wanted to tell people! I wanted to teach them about the impact of our idolatry on the heart of our Father. They had to know!
God had confirmed early on that he wanted me teaching and now he had

certainly answered my request for dreams. In receiving the revelation from this dream I was convinced that God wanted me to identify and speak to the idolatry in which people were dabbling. To call them back to a position of surrender to the one and only God.

But something still felt a little off. The whole picture still wasn't sitting quite right, so I decided to sit on the feeling and give time for the scriptures to add clarity to the dream.

My study began in the book of Hosea.

"MESSAGE IN A DREAM"

CHAPTER 4 — "MESSAGE IN A DREAM"

The Biblical book of Hosea begins with a rather discouraging message and mission provided by God to the prophet: "Go marry a promiscuous woman and have children with her."

Were I in his shoes, I would not be super eager to take on this task. In fact, I would need more than a wet fleece (Gideon's story) or a burning bush (Moses' story) to make sure this was specifically what God was telling me to do. There was, however, a great purpose behind this role and Hosea's obedience throughout his marriage to Gomer is remarkable. Upon the birth of each of their three children, God interrupts the celebration with a message to Hosea containing instructions on what to name each child and the meaning of each name:

•**Jezreel** (a son): Because I will soon punish the house of Jehu for the massacre at Jezreel, and **I will put an end to the kingdom of Israel.** In that day I will break Israel's bow in the valley of Jezreel. Layman terms: God told Hosea to name his son "God is going to destroy you."

•**Lo-Ruhamah** (a daughter): (Which means "Not Loved") For I will no longer show love to the house of Israel, that I should at all forgive them. Yet I will show love to the house of Judah; and I will save them - not by bow, sword or battle, or by horses and horsemen, but by the Lord their God. Layman terms: God told Hosea to name his daughter "You are not loved."

•**Lo-Ammi** (a son): For you are not my people, and I am not your God. Layman terms: God told Hosea to name his second son "Not my people."

Encouraging, right?

Now, there's no record of her adultery until after the children are born so I'd like to think things started off well enough. The book says "go marry a promiscuous woman" but it doesn't specify if she was already behaving in that manner. With that in mind, I can imagine Hosea wondering about the word he had been given by God and if or when it would come to pass. In fact I can imagine him living happily with Gomer and his three kids. Maybe even forgetting at times the life to which God had called him. And then one day it dawns on him.

A caravan had come to the city the previous day and he had already picked up on the flying rumors. Worse than the rumors he was hearing, Gomer hadn't come home before Hosea fell asleep the previous evening and she wasn't there when he woke up. I don't even want to imagine the questions running through his mind during that first discussion after her return home.

Worst of all, when Hosea confronts her about it, she seems comfortable with her decision and is incredulous that Hosea could be so surprised. "How could you not see this coming? I've been unhappy with you for years!" She declared.

Let's play this out for a minute... wracked with self-doubt, insecurity, distrust and fear of what's to come, Hosea's wife disavowed their marriage and her family for a life of wealth, prestige and prostitution. On top of the emotional turmoil, he's suddenly forced to address how he will raise his three children on his own.

Yes, Hosea was a prophet, but don't kid yourself. Being a prophet doesn't mean he was immune to the emotional turmoil and physical anguish of this traumatic event. For all of you who have experienced infidelity within your marriage, I apologize to resurrect these emotions. But it was clear that Israel needed to hear these words.

Are we so different today?

My imagination can run wild, so I'll do my best to paint the picture this way: Hosea lived with his wife for years prior to her infidelity. I imagine their experiences as a couple had been as authentic as any other. His love for her ran deep and was not forged out of obligation. They loved each other when times were good — but was he (her husband) not enough? Personally, I don't think that played into her decision; Gomer walked away from God long before she walked away from Hosea.

So again, I can imagine how difficult it would have been for Hosea to overcome his grief. But let's assume for a moment that he does get over it. He goes on with his career, whatever it was, and continues to raise his children and stay faithful to God's covenant — making the necessary sacrifices, observing the sabbath, etc. Meanwhile the culture around him, as it had with his wife, had melted into a debaucherous mess of self-centered pursuits.

The book of Hosea is a quick read but essentially it's the fall of man on repeat. We pursue pleasure one dopamine hit at a time at the expense of long term healthy serotonin levels. In essence, mankind did what felt good and provided an immediate response of positive reinforcement rather than making long term, sound decisions that would ultimately glorify God and produce blessings in their own lives.

Gomer was once a radiant daughter of God, the desire of his heart, but she pursued her profession and acquired vast wealth and favor. She became independent, in need of nothing. I'm sure she even had a powerful client list.

Gomer: Desired, followed, liked, paid. Sounds like she had an engaged following. Sound familiar? Not too dissimilar from the characterizations of success in today's social media world.

So one day, the man Hosea stops crying himself to sleep. Scar tissue covers the old heart wounds. Gomer had moved out long ago. The munchkins were scarred as well but they too were normalizing. Life began to carry with it a glimmer of hope. And just as this single father and his three children began creating a new pattern of life, God spoke to his prophet: "Go, show your love to your wife again, though she is loved by another man and is an adulteress." (Hosea 3:1) I imagine the dialogue going something like this:

"WHAT!?"

"No! No, Absolutely not! God, you want me to go back to her and grovel? Beg her to come back? No way! No WAY!!! God, she left me! SHE LEFT ME!

She left those three beautiful children! God, she…" and he began to moan in disbelief as God remained silent in response. "This was not part of the arrangement God!" The tears that had been long dried began flowing again as God unveiled his good purpose in Hosea's calling:

"Hosea, I brought you to this point so that you would know what I've felt as my people walk away. You are right here, in this season, with your three beautiful children and an unfaithful wife because you are my mouthpiece for this generation! Go bring home your wife and relay my message to her and to this people. Though they have treated me like Gomer has treated you, I will strip away their wealth and security. They will lose their influence and their power and be sold as slaves. Then, when all false dignity, worth and confidence has been stripped away and they have been brought to nothing because of their prostitution, I will rescue them and lead them into the wilderness. There I will speak tenderly to them and win their hearts and minds. I will woo them and the love embers we rekindle will grow into a roaring fire that will spread throughout the entire earth. My pursuit of these people is and will be relentless."

"Hosea, even now Gomer is waiting her turn in the line of slaves headed to the auction block. She is broken and has been brought to ruin. The dignity, worth and confidence she experienced because of her work has been stripped away. It was an impostor and the revelation has her in a free fall."

"Hosea, she is defeated, hopeless, crushed. Now go rescue her! Have I not appointed you? Your role was not to be a mouthpiece speaking from comfort. You are to speak life into her through your scars and tears. Do not speak of your love and devotion — SPEAK OF MINE."

"You are to remind her how much I love her and to help her find the immense value in being my daughter. The love you show her will purify her and she will learn her true worth. She is a princess. MY princess. And I have commissioned you to live out my love for my daughter. Now go rescue her!"

The book says that Hosea bought Gomer at that auction for 15 Shekels of silver and about a homer and a lethek of Barley. At the time of this writing 15 shekels (6 oz) of silver is valued at approximately $15.97/oz. A homer and lethek of Barley (430 lbs) is valued at $25.68. The sum of Gomer's exploits brought her to a place of value totaling $121.50 at auction.

Beautiful, seductive, mysterious, Gomer had left her family to pursue the pleasures of wealth and fame. In her pursuits, she lost everything. After being brought to nothing, her life had been ransomed for an approximate total of $120. She was broken. Defeated. Hopeless.

At auction, she hadn't even glanced at the bidders before the auctioneer announced 'Sold!' Yet God was about to redefine her life and her value.

Hosea submits again to God's will for his life and takes his wife back. He betroths her, wins her heart and revives her life.

God desires to do the same with each of us. Over the course of our lives we will undoubtedly encounter times of divided attention in our walk with Him. The "thief" comes to steal, kill, and destroy (John 10:10) and the first step in that destruction process begins with distraction.

If the enemy can take our eyes off God's love, he can work to focus our attention on something, anything other than Him. It's in those moments of distraction that we begin the process of forgetting who we are and how God sees and values us.

As I studied Hosea in the week following my dream, I kept hearing a recurring theme of "Relentless Pursuit." My golf dream presented me with a glimpse into the heart of our Father. The depth of passion He holds for us is immeasurable. He longs to live life with us. The intensity of that love rocked me to the core.

As I mentioned previously, it is a jealous love that craves intimacy with us: His good creation. What I thought was a lesson on idolatry turned out to be a lesson in the relentless pursuit of His beloved. Over time it became apparent that this lesson was less for the people around me and more for me. God wanted a deeper intimacy with me. He wants a deeper intimacy with you as well.

1. When we lose sight of our identity, He gently reminds us of our calling.

Often this can happen when we believe a lie or a word of criticism. When we give credence to the voices that condemn our innocence, the enemy clings to that foothold. Do not give in to those thoughts. God's love and his words remind us of our position:

> But you are God's chosen treasure - priests who are kings, a spiritual nation set apart as God's devoted ones. He called you out of darkness to experience his marvelous light and now he claims you as his very own. He did this so that you would broadcast his glorious wonders throughout the world. (1 Peter 2: 9 TPT)

When you make Jesus the lord of your life, you become a son or daughter of the King of Kings. You become a prince or a princess in God's kingdom and Holy Spirit takes up residence in his temple (you).

I think the most surprising realization of the golf dream had to have been the feelings of utter helplessness that came with the realization of my wife's infidelity. In that moment, I couldn't force her to do anything. If I pummeled the guy in my anger, she'd resent me and the resentment may have driven her further away from me, deeper into his arms. If I did nothing, their affair could have persisted indefinitely. So what is God supposed to do when the object of His affection strays from His love to find comfort in another? This is the essence of idolatry in its rawest form.

If I take an honest look at myself, I deserve the wrath of God. Period. The End. Game over. I am as guilty of breaking God's perfect law (cheating on Him) as the sun is bright and the universe is wide. AND... In that guilt, God feels a pain, an anguish, even a questioning, "Am I enough? Were my plans for you not good? Did I do something that drove you away?"

I believe God's heart broke thinking through all this — knowing that His justice demands a response. And yet, how amazing a plan... that He could take an unblemished lamb and direct every consequence for all time into that one perfect innocent. There on the cross, Jesus takes the consequence for every evil. Every vial, corrupt, adulterous thought and action that has ever been and ever will be. They all overwhelmed Jesus in the moments of his torture and God directed every ounce of justice and consequence (meant for me/you/us) into Him. All of God's righteous anger, his jealousy, and his pain were levied at Jesus in a very short window of time.

And yet I know that I earned God's wrath, his jealousy and frustration. I cheat(ed) on Him. It is my shame to bear. It is my wrath to take. **But Jesus stepped in with a change of plans.** He took it — it's no longer mine. Jesus cleared my name for all time. Yours too! When I take a moment away from the chaos of life to think about this, I get overwhelmed with an affection for my God and a gratitude for Jesus. My response in those moments is Who CAN I love? Who CAN I serve? Where CAN I go?

I think God takes great satisfaction in our love being lived out. When we transfer these realizations into our daily activity we become the salt of the earth and the light of the world that Jesus calls us to be.

2. When we get distracted by the idolatry of the world, he calls out to us.

Often the world's distractions look less like distractions than they do obligations and recreational activities. Careers, entertainment, and relationships are the new idol of choice as opposed to the traditional man made stone or wooden statue. And yet as I say that, the hours I spend focused on my phone each day (a man-made, plastic and metal, light emitting object) is staggering. If we can imagine our attention span as the digital currency I mentioned earlier, then the amount of time we spend staring at a screen for entertainment purposes is crazy expensive!

In these times, I believe the Holy Spirit cries out to us. But do I make space to listen or respond? Do you? This concept touches not only on our innocence in being distracted but also our willingness to turn away from the distractions. When we allow those distractions — those idols — to dominate our attention, our actions follow suit.

Please understand me here: I am not saying that technology is bad. Technology is a tool, it's neutral. If we don't have the discipline and understanding to turn away from the tool to respond to God's calling we'll miss a tremendous amount of goodness and life that He has planned for us. Even more, if we can't step away from the distractions to hear His call, our lives WILL begin to show signs of lukewarmness; a trait that is detestable to Jesus.

I know all that you do and I know that you are neither frozen in apathy nor fervent with passion. How I wish you were either one or the other! But because you are neither cold nor hot, but lukewarm, I am about to spit you from my mouth... All those I dearly love I unmask and train (rebuke and discipline). So repent and be eager to pursue what is right. Behold, I'm standing at the door, knocking. If your heart is open to hear my voice and you open the door within, I will come in to you and feast with you, and you will feast with me. (Revelation 3:15-16, 19-20 TPT)

Did you hear the catch in that scripture? "If your heart is **open** to hear my voice..."

We can't expect Jesus to shout over the hustle and bustle of our daily lives. We can't expect him to slap the screen out of our hands or interrupt the streaming service while we binge. The Jews wanted a forceful king to overthrow Rome. Jesus wasn't forceful. He also never coerced or begged someone to follow him.

On the flip side, he won't coddle us when we make the decision to follow. Please don't misunderstand me: following Jesus is an EVERY DAY DECISION. If we want the life to which He calls us, we can't simply choose to follow him one day and call it good. Walking with Jesus is THE MOST amazing process of restoration, fulfillment and intimacy we'll ever know but it does take our deliberate decision to step into his love and our identity every day. My encouragement to you, and the reminder to myself, is to set aside the distraction, whatever it may be, and invest your attention in the Lord:

And to the one who conquers (overcomes), I will give the privilege of sitting with me on my throne, just as I conquered and sat down with my father on his throne. (Revelation 3: 21 TPT)

I'm trying to wrap my head around how to conclude this section and I want to take you back to the idea of helplessness. Yahweh won't make us love Him and he won't force us to grasp the depth of his love. That doesn't make him helpless. God's feelings of helplessness only exist because of the restraint He exercises in allowing us to choose for ourselves whom we will love. I believe the intent of my dream was to reveal the heart of the Father and in that dream helplessness was a prevailing emotion.

Maybe helplessness is the wrong term, maybe God's vision allows him to see additional opportunities and the outcome so that despite the pain we may cause in the present, He's already hopeful for the next opportunity to woo our hearts. Again, He plays the long game.

This wooing is infectious and when we are infected by His love, we change. If that's the case then we all need to change right now in the name of Jesus, and then go change the world, right?

Nope! Stop right there! TEACHING MOMENT: If we attempt to become a force for Jesus, we will lose sight of the purpose to which we've been called and ultimately fail.

Herein lies the irony, if we would only sit, be still, and rest in His love - grasping its depth and experiencing its intimacy - we would become such a force for Him that all the world would know His goodness. But that's the paradox: **we can't become an active force for our God without resting and abiding in His love.**

In order to succeed in this thing we call discipleship, our top priority must be stepping away from the chaos of life to bask in the love of the father; recharging our spiritual batteries in His love. Working for Jesus will only lead to dogmatic rigidity, frustration, burnout. Experiencing the love of Jehovah will lead to an amazing outpouring of world changing love. It will lead to revival!

BUT WAIT! THERE'S MORE! I thought this chapter was done and then the Lord gave me some clarification on something I hadn't caught before.

Earlier in the chapter I made reference to the names of Hosea's children. They were weird names, and I wondered why God would give those names to Hosea. It seemed like God was adding insult to the injury knowing his wife would eventually walk away from him.

His son Jezreel - "I will destroy you"

His daughter Lo-Ruhamah - "You are not loved"
His second son Lo-Ammi- "You are not my people"

Consider the implications of those names. At this point God knows Israel will come back to him and he speaks prophetically about Israel's future but also about the future of Hosea's children:

> In that day I will respond declares the Lord — I will respond to the skies, and they will respond to the earth; and the earth will respond to the grain, and the new wine and the olive oil and they will respond to Jezreel. (God tells Hosea he is going to bless his first born son with bountiful harvests and restore his standing)

> I will plant her for myself in the land; I will show my love to the one I called 'Not my loved one.' (God says he's going to show love to Hosea's daughter who was called 'Not Loved.')

> I will say to those called 'Not my people,' 'You are my people'; and they will say, 'You are my God.' (Hosea 2:20-23)

God was telling Hosea that his children would be completely restored after the hardship they were about to endure. Now, Hosea's message was originally intended for the people of Israel. They would be restored after they strayed from him, pursuing idols and prostituting themselves to foreign gods.

He would allow them to experience all the depths of their depravity. It would begin with the benefits from their activity but eventually it would run its course and leave them worse than they had been before it all began. They would be destitute, broken, left with nothing. At that point, God would sweep them away and woo them. He would betroth them and win their hearts back. He would restore their position and give them back their dignity.

God has the same game plan in mind for you and me. When we stray, he won't interrupt our plans but he will let us experience the depravity that comes with those decisions. Then, when we're broken and defeated and we cry out for him, he's ready to swoop us up, win our hearts back and

establish our position as his sons and daughters.

Now, tell me THAT won't preach! I was ready! I was ready to live out my calling and go teach the people the lesson God had just revealed to me. At least, that's what I thought...

"...WAIT FOR IT!"

CHAPTER 5 — "...WAIT FOR IT!"

Folsom Field in Boulder Colorado is one of the most majestic venues in all of college football. There's really not a bad seat in the house. The exterior of this structure matches the architectural designs and stonework of all the other buildings at the University - sandstone walls with limestone trim, red tile roofs and black wrought iron accents on all the gates and access points. The field runs north to south with the old Dal Ward athletic center at the north end and a U-shaped student section to the south.

Any seat on the west side of the field will have shade in the hot afternoon sun and if the seats are high enough, the spectator will be able to look beyond the campus to the beginning touches of the Great Plains. (Okay, I'm making that sound a bit more majestic than it is. These are the best seats early in the season when the weather is still hot and the sun is blasting down on the majority of the stadium. The shade, provided by the adjacent field house, is a welcome relief to the exposure at 5300+ feet.) This is where most of the boosters sit. These are the pricey tickets.

From the east side of the stadium the view is significantly better. The backdrop of the campus against the abrupt formation of the Flat Irons, at the base of the Rocky Mountains, creates awe inspiring moments, especially when the Buffs win. If you're going to sit anywhere in Folsom, this is the place to be, just not without a hat and sunscreen in the early part of the season.

But the best place to be in that stadium, perhaps on a warm September evening when the crowd is in a frenzy and the season is about to begin, is on the field. Prior to kickoff, the stadium lights turn on well before the sun begins its descent. Players from both teams warm up on their respective sides of the field. Fans stream into the stadium; some finding their seats, some loitering in the aisles taking in the overwhelming sight. The speaker system blasts upbeat music while the band attempts to compete with their more classical warm up routine. There's a general buzz in the air and with it an electric excitement that charges each player, coach, or spectator in a different way. The smell of the grass, the tape, the pads — it's all been locked away into memory after years of rehearsal.

My final season playing for Colorado was in 2005. I had an epic five year journey with many swings both positive and negative. I wasn't a key player by any means (I didn't see the field until my fourth year) but I can vividly remember that first experience running down the field on a kick-off.

Back to 2018... God had given me two dreams early in the year and I was thoroughly convinced that the time was coming for me to launch into a season of teaching. I had dinner with a friend and shared with him the confirming word about teaching and the lesson filled dream(s). His advice was "then you'd better prepare."

By that point though I was up for anything — starting a small group, speaking to the church community on a weeknight gathering, or even speaking on a Sunday morning. I didn't really care, I was up for any of it, I was just eager to start. I drafted notes on my study of Hosea and rehearsed the storyline of my golf dream but no opportunity to teach presented itself. I was waiting on the Lord, but it didn't appear that my desire to teach was anywhere near the front of the queue.

I'm sure every one of you reading this would fancy yourself a patient person if asked. I can imagine it, but I know enough after being married 14 years and having three children to say that I possess the potential to be patient. I'm selective about when I'll let that skill 'outta the bag.' My shortcomings in this regard will not be discussed at present. For now, what you need to know is that I was ready. And I hoped that God was seeing my preparation. What presented itself was not a speaking platform, but another dream.

The dream started on that perfect evening in Folsom Field as described earlier. I was completely enthralled with the scene. The game was about to start, the crowd was in a frenzy, the band was playing, and the announcer was saying something over the loudspeaker. I was ready to go in for the opening kickoff, but for some reason I wasn't slotted to play that day. In fact, I remember specifically that there were two guys on the depth chart ahead of me. It didn't matter though, I was ready. I sought out my special teams coach and when I found him, I told him that I needed to go in. He replied simply, "Hammond, you're not ready."

In hindsight, my assertion is rather comical because there are no surprise changes to the game plan on game day. The depth chart has usually been set for the entire week. Additionally, the offense scripts (plans) the first 10-15 plays of the game and runs them regularly throughout the week so that by game time, they can execute the plan without a huddle or play call from the sideline. Again, there are no surprises. So, it would be ludicrous for a player, who happens to be third on the depth chart for any position, to assert his readiness to go in. At best it would be presumptuous and arrogant. At worst it would reveal a lack of intelligence, and that's putting it nicely.

Apparently, none of this mattered in my dream. I objected to his assertion. "Coach you've seen me train! You know I'm strong enough. You know I'm fast enough! We've been over the cues. I know what players to key in on after the kick and we know exactly what they're going to run. Coach, it's only kick-off and you know I'm ready!"

"Matt, settle down. I can't put you in. You're not ready... You're not wearing any pants."

I had already been forming my rebuttal to his objection but his statement stumped me, stopped me cold. Speaking of cold, I looked down and could immediately feel a gentle breeze on my thighs.

"You have got to be kidding me!" I was wearing a helmet, shoulder pads and a jersey. I had my gloves strapped, my ankles were taped, my socks pulled high and cleats laced up. I was definitely ready to go, except that I DIDN'T HAVE ON ANY FREAKING PANTS! I was standing in front of 55,000+ people without my pants and I wasn't even embarrassed, I was just pissed! How could I have overlooked something so important!?

I was ready to play and although my coach knew I was ready, he wouldn't play me over a stupid technicality like 'football pants'. Not that I blame him. As frustrated as I was, I knew it wasn't an option. I ran into the locker room yelling, "Where are my pants!?" Then I woke up.

Again, I laid there in bed, staring at a dark ceiling, brow furrowed trying to connect the dots on this one. What in the world was God saying?

This dream didn't elicit the chaotic emotion I experienced previously but it did give me pause. I pulled out my journal and wrote the dream out, asking for God to give me insight. Prior to the arrival of any epiphany, I dozed off.

The following morning I replayed the dream in my mind and shared it with Lauren. We were en route to church that morning and as I recounted the events that played out and processed what was happening, I got my download. Holy smokes, I am not ready!

When I was 14 years old, I attended a church camp that took me and 250 other campers and counselors to Lake Shasta, CA. We rented 10-15 house boats and filled our days with jet skis, wake boards, inner-tubes, and Life Flight helicopters.

Yes, you read that correctly. That year, life flight was called in twice to our camp. One kid had a gnarly crash on his wake board and somehow the fin from under the board slashed his face; he was done for the week. The other helicopter trip was due to a broken arm or leg (I can't remember which) and while it seems like a bit of an overkill, it happened nonetheless. Then we proceeded to crash and sink a jet ski. Fortunately it sank in just three feet of water. Then a camper, who had snuck alcohol in with his bags, got drunk and punched a counselor. He too was sent home. (I know this all sounds a bit exaggerated but I swear it all happened) Then a ski boat I happened to be riding in caught fire while we were out tubing. The inboard engine overheated and an oil leak combusted. With plenty of time to spare, we threw on life jackets and bailed overboard to await the fireboats. It was a bit surreal to be floating in the water, watching flames leap out the back of the boat.

When the week was over and we got back to the docks, we had earned a nickname around the lake as the Church Camp from Hell. However, all that excitement aside, it was a really great trip, and I remember one evening specifically.

After a massive bonfire and worship session, we were drifting off to sleep in our sleeping bags on the roof of our houseboat. The stars were incredible and I remember a very specific feeling came over me — I was supposed to be a voice for the Lord. Specifically, I was meant to speak to people on a large scale about Jesus. I was going to be an evangelist.

Aaaaaannnnnd, back to 2018 — God had given me a confirmation that I was going to be a teacher. I had asked Him to begin speaking to me through dreams and he had now responded with three.

Dream 1: He showed me that something needed to be removed from my character in order to do something great for Him.

Dream 2: He gave me a view into the effect our idolatry has on his heart and taught me that regardless of our infidelity, he is relentlessly pursuing our hearts. (This was to be my first real message.)

Dream 3: He had informed me that I was not yet ready for the task at hand.

In my football dream I was third on the depth chart. That doesn't bode well for playing time, but I was convinced I was ready to go in. It's not the first time I have gotten a bit ahead of myself. At the age of 10, I took my first Tae-Kwon-Do test and graduated from white to yellow belt. Upon completion I asked Master Shin if I could just memorize the form test for the black belt evaluation and take the test a week or two later. If I could jump from white to yellow with the amount of training I had put in, how hard would it be to jump to very top? (I'll claim ignorance here, not arrogance.)

So yes, I have a tendency to dive into the deep end before knowing how to swim. It seemed in this case that the Lord was informing me that mindset wouldn't go over well in what was coming.

But what was coming? Why was God now holding me back? I felt ready, but there was the whole part about not having any pants. Pants were a definite necessity; if not for the padding they held, then at least for the decency they provided. Ha! I still chuckle at the idea of jogging onto the field without them. But what were my pants? (figuratively speaking of course) And how was I supposed to find them?

So here's the takeaway. God wants to partner with each of us throughout the course of our lives and on into eternity. (For reference, take a look at the creation story and the responsibility he gives to Adam and Eve.) To this end He's gifted us with skills and abilities that He knows will be useful in His kingdom.

Part of walking with Jesus is understanding who He made us to be and what He has called us to do.

But while making the decision to walk in our calling is a fantastic first step, it may not mean that we're ready run full speed in the race to which God is calling us. I'm sure I'm not the only one in this boat, (or maybe "on this field" is the better analogy) but often times I want to leap ahead in the work/calling before I'm ready. Unfortunately that leads to some challenging lessons and also makes us second guess God's calling on our life.

I need to walk before I can run, even though I'm confident God's plan includes me sprinting (eventually). In the case of my dream, I felt the Lord was telling me I either needed to start shedding the baggage I had picked up over the course of my life or begin developing the raw talents with which he's blessed me. Or maybe it was both. Regardless, I can't play the game without pants, and I wouldn't recommend it to you either.

The word potential can be a double-edged sword. I personally despise the word because it speaks to undeveloped ability. But consider which of the following phrases you would prefer to hear about yourself:

-She/He has so much potential.
-She/He had so much potential.

There's a stark contrast there. One speaks to raw talent needing to be honed before its valued. The other speaks to a waste of that talent. Neither makes me happy but I'd much rather hear that I have potential. The difference between the two is **time.**

God has placed a calling on your life, just as he has placed a calling on mine.

But it's still up to you and it's still up to me to develop our talent so we can eventually step into our calling. Recently I heard a message from Pastor Mike Todd of Transformation Church. In it he said that people want the prophetic word, but they're not willing to do the prophetic work. That one hits home for many of us! How are you spending your time? Are you intentional about the development of your gifting(s)?

I look back at the dream now with an understanding that I was not yet equipped to step into the role that God had/has for me. I'm so very grateful that He got my attention with the dream because I'd be a fool to attempt to walk into my calling without developing the potential/talent he's provided.

This line of thinking is not intended to cast shame and/or guilt. The enemy would use those feelings to drive you away from the Lord. Knowing this tactic, don't allow it to affect you. Fight it and draw near to the Lord.

The purpose of these words is to remind you of the heights to which you have been called and to focus your attention on developing the talents that will partner with the Lord in getting you there! If you're reading these words, it means there is yet time to step into that calling and develop your potential. At this very moment you may feel unprepared (or worse, over-prepared) for the massive project he has for you. Or maybe you think your life has run its course, that there can't possibly be another purpose or adventure for you (study the life of Caleb if you relate with this feeling).

But to reiterate a previous point, we are a work in process. Holy Spirit wants to hone each of us into tools that can be wielded for His kingdom and our collective good! And hear me on this... We can't sharpen ourselves! The best thing we can do is to lean into His goodness and His love and allow Holy Spirit to guide our steps. He'll bring us to people who can sharpen us and then position us for the work.

Ask Him to lead you in developing your talents so your adventure can begin. As I'll share later, the development process won't always be easy, but it is most certainly for our good and for the good of His kingdom.

But seriously, where were my pants!?

"THE DAMN DAM"

CHAPTER 6 — "THE DAMN DAM"

My throat was suddenly tight. It hurt to make sound and it felt constricted in a way that I hadn't ever experienced. I stood there in the second row of the church building — palms up, eyes closed, tears streaming down my face. God wanted me to go deeper. I wanted to go deeper. But something was holding me back and whatever it was needed to be dealt with. I'll get to that in a minute.

In late 2017, I had decided to go fishing with a friend of mine. It was early on a wet fall day with overcast skies and the cool air felt sharp against any exposed skin. Leaves had already begun falling from the trees and covered the ground with a fragrant carpet of brown and yellow, damp and padded under our feet. I don't remember saying much on that hike because we had a pent up anticipation of our arrival. Our fishing spot was/is epic in its beauty and the hole itself is overly generous in the fish it surrenders; I was excited to see what we'd end up taking home that day.

The hike through the trees was short-lived, though it always seems longer when we think back on it, and the river was flowing beautifully when we arrived. As we began setting up, I heard the familiar sound of the rushing water but also a general commotion upstream. I looked up to see what appeared to be a small construction project.

We weren't near any major cities so it was a bit odd to see something of this nature (pun intended) in the middle of the woods. I walked along the bank toward the commotion wanting to get a better look and as I approached I realized it wasn't a construction project but a small fishing operation.

There were temporary spotlights on both sides of the river used to illuminate the area for night work. A platform had been constructed across the river making it appear to be dam like in nature, but it wasn't holding back any water. In fact, water was flowing swiftly around four steel pillars driven into the riverbed with a metal netting strewn between each pillar. The netting had been constructed to permit the flow of water but corral any fish making their way downstream. As we watched, every few minutes one of the workers on the platform would pull a large net full of fish from the water and empty its contents onto the surface of the platform. The fish flopped around for a time and eventually went still. One of the workers happened to notice a large sturgeon that had been ripped from the river and threw it over the ledge back into the free-flowing side.

They were gill netting the entire river! Piles of dead fish lay motionless on the platform and suddenly the smell of rot and decay was overwhelming. I stood on the river bank stunned, wondering how this could all be happening.

Regardless of our choice of bait that day, we wouldn't be catching anything. As beautiful as the river looked as it flowed downstream, there was zero life in it. To make matters worse, I knew that what was happening was immoral, deplorable, but I was helpless to stop it and somehow I knew that some governing body had permitted the activity. I woke up in confusion and like before, wrote out the dream.

There must be something sacred about Saturday evenings because Holy Spirit had queued up another dream just in time for me to process its meaning and gather our family for worship the next morning. **What was God saying?** As I unpacked the dream, again en route to church, I was able to draw out some of its embedded meaning.

My friend (Jesus) and I were planning to spend the day together fishing. We had our spot picked out and had been there many times before. It was a picture-perfect setting. Fallen logs and large boulders created white water currents and eddies and there were deep areas near the eddies and back-flows where the fish would be resting while they made their way upriver to spawn.

Shallow water near the banks made for a perfect landing from which to cast or even take a dip as the heat rose late in the day. Despite the beauty of our spot, the river lacked life. It was stale, sterile. It was an image of my own spiritual life.

Maybe you can relate. A shiny exterior with a sterile interior? Anyone? Bueller?

More recently I've gotten the sense that revival in the midst of our chaos is a theme God is highlighting throughout His kingdom. Chaos, being a very general term can manifest in many ways: concern over careers, relationships, money, health, etc. All that aside, I believe God is intensely interested in our response to him in the midst of this chaos.

Consider Job… God allowed Job to be tested far beyond what many of us will ever experience. He allowed it as evidence to Satan that Job's faithfulness had nothing to do with the blessed life in which he lived.

Have you been faithful in the midst of your chaos? Think about that for a minute.

It's a tough and pointed question but regardless of your answer, I believe God is working through the chaos of your life **to remind you of His faithfulness.** In my dream, the dam represented a powerful snare that prevented Holy Spirit life from flowing freely. I wanted that to change. God wanted that to change. He wants it to change in your story as well!

The river of my life and yours is intended to be filled with abundant life. Holy Spirit life! The kind of life that makes a fishing trip with the Lord an enjoyable day! Towards the end of the book of Mark, Jesus tells his disciples:

> "As you go into all the world, preach openly the wonderful news of the gospel to the entire human race! Whoever believes the good news and is baptized will be saved, and whoever does not believe the good news will be condemned. And these miracle signs will accompany those who believe: They will drive out demons in the power of my name. They will speak in tongues. They will be supernaturally protected from snakes and from drinking anything poisonous. And they will lay hands on the sick and heal them." (Mark 16: 15-18 TPT)

I had begun pondering Jesus' statement more frequently over the previous months as people were walking out those gifts in our new church culture. There were regular prayers for healing and in those prayers, people were telling spirits to depart in Jesus' name.

Why hadn't I ever experienced this before? In the 15 years leading up to this point I had definitely focused heavily on the baptism side of the Mark 16 scripture, but never the miraculous signs that Jesus says will follow those who believe. Did Holy Spirit really want me to start laying hands on people for healing? Speaking in new languages? Driving out demons?

We had been attending our new church home for nearly three months by this time and every weekend seemed to bring with it an emotional flood of tears during worship. I knew something good was happening each time and every week I craved that intimacy with God, but I also looked forward to the days when I would be able to get through a Sunday morning without bloodshot eyes and a runny nose. Maybe then I'd be able to minister to someone else.

Brant, our worship pastor was doing his thing the Sunday morning following my dream — which generally included a massive karaoke worship party to incredible live music. (Side note: I don't think I've ever been around a more talented group of musicians. We're forever ruined if we go to worship at another church… it's Bethel, it's Hillsong. It's that good!) At any rate, Brant had received a word from the Lord and shared it with us during the bridge. At that time, despite beginning to hear from the Lord myself, I still was hesitant when someone said they heard something from the Lord.

As the band played through the bridge, Brant began sharing a message the Spirit put on his heart. He said he felt the spirit of God calling people deeper - deep crying out to deep. Specifically, he said that as we went deeper we would experience breakthrough in our intimacy with the Father.

Now I won't say that this word was as powerful as the first confirmation, but I had just experienced my own revelatory dream and wondered about its correlation with this word.

Even that word he used **"breakthrough"** caught my attention, in light of the dam that was killing off the spirit-filled life. I was ready for that breakthrough. The dream weighed heavily on my mind as he spoke and I began to visualize the dam being destroyed by an overwhelming wave of water. As he kicked back up into the chorus I opened my palms, closed my eyes and took a deep breath to join him in song… and then it happened. My vocal cords just locked up and I couldn't sing. And that's unusual.

I'm not much of a dancer so I don't bounce around in worship. I'm also not prone to shaking my head or waving flags. I just sing. Loud. Occasionally with arms raised.

Choir was one of my favorite high school classes. So now, naturally, I listen for the chords, find the notes and belt the words as loud as I possibly can. Only occasionally, when the song hits a high note and my voice cracks, ·

straining to match pitch, do I pity the people within earshot.

On this particular Sunday, after my dream, I so badly wanted breakthrough. But my vocal cords constricted and I couldn't make a sound to save my life. The emotion of that moment was overwhelming and I just stood there feeling stupid — palms up, mouth open, tears flowing down my face. I was begging God for new depth, asking him to destroy the dam, trying repeatedly to sing, but mute as a mime.

Now, from a physiological perspective, I understand what happened to my body. As I mentioned, the emotion of the moment was intense and I'm sure that just like any child has difficulty talking while they're crying over a skinned knee, I too was having difficulty producing sound. I get it.

But the metaphor of my dream (a life killing dam) was not lost on me in that moment. Apparently, the damn dam was stronger than I had anticipated.

With no breakthrough and no clear direction on how to proceed, I was left to wrestle with this dream. I prayed, I fasted, and I journaled all the while begging God for insight. I replayed the scene over and over in my mind and eventually I came to focus on the four pillars driven into the riverbed. They were the foundation for this life-sucking operation and if I was going to go deeper with God, they had to go.

I don't understand why, but I had a sense that my reluctance towards the supernatural was preventing me from experiencing a supernatural breakthrough. It started in small spurts, but over time, I began learning more about demonic forces, how they work and how our agreement with their suggestions empowers them in our lives. (Side note - An amazingly entertaining and insightful read on this topic is Laura Gallier's series The Delusion… go read those too!)

With that in mind, I began assessing our living situation, my family dynamic, the relationships with my work colleagues and piece by piece, it all started making sense.

In September of 2017, we sold our farm and moved to the suburbs, closer to my wife's work. That move was made for a number of reasons but originated mostly out of my fear of financial ruin. We were stretched thin when we bought the place, but with the arrival of our third child and all the financial implications parenting brings, my anxiety began to rise on a regular basis.

Although deep in my gut I felt it was a mistake, we signed the paperwork to sell. In that moment, **I stepped into alignment with Anxiety and Fear** and there was no changing my mind.

There in the suburbs, in our temporary rental, we squeezed ourselves and our three kiddos into a two bed, one bathroom home - less than a thousand square feet. This was to be for no more than three months and yet I am sitting in the dining room of that very house typing these words nearly two years after our arrival.

There are definite positives to this place though. Deep cleaning the entire house takes one hour tops! The perceived downside when we first moved in was that there was no way we could possibly host people in our home and I began to think, "If we had a larger home we'd be able to..." **And that ushered in Discontentment.** Without knowing it, I had shaken hands with this smooth-talking demonic force and it prevented me from wanting to use the home as a blessing for other people.

After six months in the house (we now refer to it as 'the cottage' or our 'tiny house') I became more discontent with our setup and began regretting the sale of our farm. I was frustrated that my emotions so drastically affected my decisions and led our family to this point. I wanted my kids to have the same kind of upbringing that I had - at the very least to have their own rooms.

My business had been successful for the previous four years... on what had I been spending the money? Where had it gone? Lauren had a fantastically successful career at Fortune 500 company that carries a prestigious, global brand... Our life should not feel like a dead-end in our mid-thirties. **Hello Expectations!**

I began agreeing with the voices whispering in my ears that I should be farther along. Surely my peers from high school and college were much better off than we were. My parents were lightyears ahead of me when they were my age. What was I doing? What were we doing?

As I replayed the storyline of the dream, I began to see that the principalities and demonic forces of this world were having a tremendous influence on my life.

Now I know I just lost some of you to that sort of hocus-pocus Christianity again, but consider that Paul, writing to the church in Ephesus, says:

> Your hand to hand combat is not with human beings, but with the highest principalities and authorities operating in rebellion under the heavenly realms. For they are a powerful class of demon-gods and evil spirits that hold this dark world in bondage. (Ephesians 6: 12 TPT)

I had shaken hands with spiritual powers by allowing Discontentment, Fear, Anxiety, and the Expectations of my life to dictate how I would think and behave and the Lord eventually revealed that these were the four pillars of the dam.

It wasn't a breakthrough yet, but at least I knew what I was up against. The scripture in Hebrews kept ringing in my mind, reminding me of the growth that needed to occur: "But we are certainly not those who are held back by fear and perish; we are among those who have faith and experience true life!" (Hebrews 10: 39 TPT)

Whether or not we feel it, God desires to take us to a deeper level of intimacy with Him. But perhaps, like I did, you also feel like you're being held back. Maybe it's not a tightening of the throat in worship that's needed to wake you up to that notion, maybe you just sense it in your gut.

I asked God, pleaded with Him to show me what was holding me back and he gave me a dream about four sins that I had unknowingly agreed with; four sins that were killing a spirit filled life. The character flaws were crippling my breakthrough and preventing a deeper level of intimacy with God, Jesus, and Holy Spirit.

The question I would pose to you is this: Have you asked the Lord to reveal what (if anything) is holding you back?

But more importantly... do you really want to know the answer?

"ANOTHER CONFIRMATION"

CHAPTER 7 — "ANOTHER CONFIRMATION"

Discontentment - Dissatisfaction with one's circumstances.

Fear - An unpleasant emotion caused by the belief that someone or something is dangerous, likely to cause pain or a threat.

Anxiety - A feeling of worry, nervousness, or unease, typically about an imminent event or something with an uncertain outcome.

Expectation - A belief that someone will or should achieve something.

I couldn't quite understand how these four emotions were affecting my walk with the Lord but I made the conscious decision to address each one as soon as possible. I also couldn't figure out how these 'pillars' had been erected in the river of my life in the first place. To gain some momentum (and confidence that I could conquer each) I decided to address discontentment first. It seemed easy enough: change my perspective and show gratitude for the simple blessings. I decided to take an inventory of everything happening in my life and thank God for placing me right here in this space. This literal space, our cottage, our tiny home.

Prior to selling the farm, we had grown accustomed to regularly hosting 15-20 people every weekend. The house wasn't a monster, but it was 3000+ sq ft. It had four bedrooms and three bathrooms and sat on nearly 15 acres. There was a huge deck off the back of the house with a detached garage and two barns. There was a year-round creek that ran through the property and a very large pond that supported a family of Nutria along with a number of other water-loving species. We had steers, pigs, chickens, goats, and a dog. It was a great place and we had more than enough room.

As I mentioned earlier, after selling the farm we temporarily landed in a small house near Lauren's office. While I appreciated the financial relief and the proximity to anything we could need (store, highways, schools, etc.), we were crammed in the little two bedroom, one bathroom, 961 sq ft home. If it weren't for a fantastic experience living in Amsterdam in 2011, where homes are small, I think we would have gone crazy very early on in our stay.

Around that time someone told us that we have the gift of hospitality. It hadn't hit us until then but it was true... we loved, and still love, exercising that gift! But this house made it difficult. Our dinner table had the capacity to seat ten but it was rarely stretched to seat more than the five of us in this new space. Even with one additional person, the dining room felt uncomfortably small.

I had to pray through this new discomfort. That may sound silly but I stopped inviting people to our home because it became embarrassing to explain our circumstance. In addition to living in the cottage, my day to day line of work is in the real estate industry. I'm regularly touring people's homes and I get to see some of the more beautiful properties in Portland and SW Washington. Nearly every day I walked out of these properties imagining my family living in something similar. Then I would drive across town, pick up my kids from school and daycare and arrive home at our "tiny house."

"Thank you, Lord, for our home. Thank you, Lord, for my family. Thank you, Lord, for..." You get the idea. If I was going to pull this pillar from the bedrock of the river and allow life to flow again it had to start with gratitude.

> Rejoice always, pray continually, give thanks in all circumstances; for this is God's will for you in Christ Jesus. (1 Thessalonians 5: 16-18)

> Give thanks to the Lord for he is good, His Love endures forever. Give thanks to the God of gods: His love endures forever. Give thanks to the Lord of lords: His love endures forever. (Psalm 136: 1-3)

For nearly a solid week I focused intently on thanking God for every component of my life. More than anything I thanked Father God for our home and, wouldn't you know, by the end of the week my contentment began to rise. It wasn't a ten rating, but it was no longer at a two or three either. I wasn't ready to begin another house church at the cottage, but I began opening up to the idea of having people over for dinner.

Throughout this time though, God's voice had gone quiet in my sleep. I was sure he was still working but I stopped dreaming for what felt like an uncomfortable length of time. Was God delaying further communication until I addressed the dam issues? It began feeling like a quest style video game but I couldn't believe that God worked like that.

At any rate, discontentment in my heart was being addressed as best as I could manage but there were still the three other pillars: fear, anxiety, and expectations. I knew better than to go at these pillars lightly. I thought discontentment would be an easy fix because its presence was a matter of perspective. Change the perspective, remove the pillar. Simple. The other three were a little more intimidating and I didn't know how to even begin addressing them.

I don't remember the timeline on the series of events that followed but we were still in the Spring of 2018, I remember that much. Sunday had come again and we were comfortably settling into our routine of attending church. Worship would be followed by a message and an additional song before we'd hang out with a new group of friends that afternoon.

Jenny, one of the ministry leaders at the church had spoken that morning on entering into God's rest. It was an interesting lecture on rest not being a position or place but a mindset that was infused into our body, soul, and spirit. It was good. I didn't feel like rest was elusive in my walk with Jesus but maybe there was a connection between rest and the three pillars I was still addressing. I typed out the following notes on my phone that morning: 'The three things preventing me from entering God's rest: **Fear, Anxiety, Expectations.**' She finished her discussion and the worship team came back to the stage to close out our time.

I don't remember what song played but I remember a guy walking to the front and standing at the right side of the stage at the start of the song. He had a black lanyard on his neck that said 'Prayer' and not five seconds passed before I heard Holy Spirit whisper, "He needs to pray for you."

"Nah, I'm good." I thought.

Another ten seconds passed and I heard it again while singing. "He needs to pray for you."

"No thanks. I'm doing just fine." Walking to the stage and attracting the eyes of the crowd was not my style.

Jenny hadn't invited people up for an altar call or prayer requests. I didn't want to make a scene and I've never been one to seek the inadvertent attention of the crowd. I'll stand up to teach or even interrupt things when

I receive a word of knowledge for the group, but I'm not going to be the guy who draws attention to himself while having an intimate moment with my God. That's for Him and me. No one else.

Another ten seconds passed and I heard it again. "He needs to pray for you."

> "Today, if you hear his voice, do not harden your hearts as you did in Meribah, as you did that day at Massah in the desert, where your fathers tested and tried me, though they had seen what I did. For forty years I was angry with that generation; I said, 'They are a people whose hearts go astray, and they have not known my ways.' So I declared on oath in my anger, 'They shall never enter my REST.'" (Psalm 95: 8-11)

I wanted to hear God's voice and direction through dreams. Had he not given me dreams in response? That Sunday morning wasn't the first time I had felt a prompting from Holy Spirit? Had I heard Him before and hardened my heart?

The Psalm mentions Meribah (meaning 'quarreling') and Massah (meaning 'testing') in reference to the Israelites grumbling against God and Moses in Exodus 17. At that point in Israeli history, God had brought the plagues upon Egypt to deliver the Israelites out of Pharaoh's hand. He (God) had parted the waters of the Red Sea. He brought them Manna to eat each morning and water from a rock. When they complained of those provisions, He gave them meat (quail)... a delicacy on most modern menus. What more was needed for the people to be content and trust that He really was their good shepherd? More poignantly, what more did I need Him to do to earn my trust?

God had provided the Israelites with food and yet they continued to doubt his provision. Worse, they complained about it. They got thirsty and rather than ask or wait patiently for water, they quarreled with Moses (His servant) and grumbled against God for His lack of provision. Their **discontentment** more than likely had to do with a rational **fear** that their needs would not be met; and it's not difficult to imagine how **anxiety** levels could have risen in the camp when the people began talking about their fears with one another. Add to that their **expectations** of freedom, fueled by the memories they carried from Egypt of eating 'fish (at no cost), cucumbers, melons, leeks, onions, and garlic' (Numbers 11:5).

Hmmm... that's weird. The Israelites were **discontent, afraid, anxious**, and carried with themselves heavy **expectations** on how their life would unfold in their freedom. When these didn't align they complained to Moses and blamed God. My dream had 4 pillars that were the basis of killing off the Holy Spirit life within me: Discontentment, Fear, Anxiety, and Expectations.

Even now, as I evaluate these four sins, I see that the root struggle was and is trusting that God is who He says He is; trusting that He is a loving father, a good shepherd. He knows my needs. He knows what's best for me. Did I trust him? Would I trust Him? Remember the word I received in that first bible study... God told me that I was a 'scared little boy afraid to trust his father's will.'

"Fine, Fine!" I thought. "He can pray for me, but **after** worship is over." I had relented and would ask for prayer but in a way that wouldn't draw attention. My way.

I didn't even let the voice finish when it came again ten seconds later. "He needs to pr..."

I was already in the aisle walking towards the stage. This was not a hesitant stroll. I walked with purpose and I wasn't particularly pleased to be interrupted again or to be interrupting the worship of rows of people as I walked by. If I'm honest, I was pissed - again! This was NOT what I wanted to be doing that morning but Holy Spirit wouldn't shut up about it.

I walked up to the guy, Bryce, who is now a good friend, and shouted in his ear over the music, "Hey man, you're supposed to pray for me."

"Great," he said. "What can I pray for?" In most cases, people walk forward in need of prayer and agreement about something heavy going on in life but I didn't think I had anything needing prayer. I was just told to go, so I went. I certainly wasn't about to tell him that I heard a voice telling me he needed to pray for me.

"Nope. You don't get that." I said. "You just need to pray for me."
Bryce gave me a quizzical look — probably due to my curt reply. (Again, I was pissed.) He nodded, placed his hand on my shoulder and dove in.

He began praying about the word we had just heard from the pulpit... prayer that I would have expected from anyone that morning. Then Bryce went quiet for a few seconds.

When he started back up, his demeanor had changed. Instead of praying in generalities the way I anticipated he would — Bryce got very specific. I don't remember the prayer verbatim, but it went something like this:

"God, I feel like Matt is dealing with some things; like there are some things weighing him down, keeping him from living out a life you have planned. God, it seems like Matt is dealing with fear..."

WHAT!?

I quickly glanced up to look at Bryce but his head was still bowed and his eyes were closed. So I dropped my head again. There's no way that he could've seen what I had written... my phone was off and he hadn't sat by me during the lesson.

Bryce continued, "...and the fear along with the anxiety that accompanies it is affecting his ability to see clearly in his decision-making process."

I ground my teeth together, my throat got tight and my eyes started watering. How in the world did this guy know that fear and anxiety were even on my radar?

"I'm also feeling that he's placed some expectations on himself..."

And then I lost it.

"...that he's taken on some expectations from his father and that those expectations are really heavy burdens. God, I ask that you would remove these barriers in the name of Jesus and allow Matt to enter into your rest."

By this time I was sobbing in agreement with him in prayer. Not five minutes prior I had written down those exact three things and this guy, who barely knew my name had nailed them — IN ORDER! I don't recall having any expectations as I strolled to the front that morning. But I now believe Holy Spirit wanted to confirm His voice over my own inner monologue. This was the second time he had used someone else as a confirmation and it served as a reminder: If I pay attention, **I can hear His voice.**

Allow me to speak a simple word of truth in your direction... **You can too!**

"CANCER"

CHAPTER 8 — "CANCER"

I have a fairly common form of cancer. If not treated, I probably won't
make it. The doctors would say this form of cancer is inoperable because
it's grown pervasively for years. Radiation won't work and while Chemo will
make me sick, it won't necessarily do anything to affect the cancer itself.
My diet won't play a role either. There have been some studies assessing the
impact of fasting on cancer and while I believe that fasting may be one of the
most effective ways to combat this disease, I also really enjoy eating. So, for
now, my game plan is to pray and fast when I can handle it. All that said, I
believe the Lord can provide a miracle.

We were now in March of 2018 and I had received four dreams from the
lord in the span of two months. Decades had passed since I had dreamt this
way and I began expectantly waiting for the next vision. Meanwhile, I was still
trying to 'find my pants' and 'remove the pillars' from my riverbed.

The next dream I had, number five, was by far the shortest. In the dream
I had a cancer in my spine and the only way to fight it was to insert a
small metal chip into my spinal column between disks seven and eight.
After writing out the dream and asking Lauren to inspect my back the
next morning, I pretty much forgot about it. But that dream carried more
significance than I realized at the time. Hopefully my explanation of it's
impact in this chapter will make sense.

Dream number six arrived a couple of days later with another marriage
testing scenario. In this dream I was married to Lauren and our marriage
was fantastic; in fact, it was very similar to our marriage now, except for
the fact that I also happened to be dating another woman. To top it off, this
new relationship felt like a perfectly acceptable arrangement, despite the
"exclusivity clause" in my wedding vows.

The setting of the dream seemed to shift rapidly while I spoke to people
about the other woman... a living room, a coffee shop, and a bar amongst a
few others. I was only in each place for a few moments but while there, the
people I spoke with were really excited that I was about to start seriously

dating this other woman. We weren't living in the same geographical location, but we had decided to visit each other in an effort to move the relationship forward.

Toward the end of the dream, I was in my car driving in my neighborhood while on the phone with the other woman. We were talking through the details of our upcoming visit when I realized I was married — happily married. In fact, Lauren was sitting in the passenger seat right next to me! Before that point I had clearly forgotten about the sanctity of my marriage. So when it hit me, I sat there in the car (still dreaming at this point), thinking about how wrong I had been. I realized that Lauren knew I was pursuing this other woman while still married to her. It was as if my wife had been present with me at every meeting place where others had encouraged the relationship.

She observed everything but hadn't objected, overheard every detail but never voiced her pain; she knew I was in the wrong but never condemned me. Rather, she patiently waited for me to arrive at the truth: I was hurting her and our relationship.

When the realization hit, I was so convicted! I remember abruptly cutting off the conversation and ending the relationship with the other woman. And then I woke up.

The following quote is a journal entry I penned after writing out the dream:

"I believe God is showing me his level of patience. He won't always rescue me from the consequences of my mistakes, but he waits in anticipation for me to come to my senses and return to him. God is patient, and he has laid out for me what is right and wrong. When I make the wrong decisions, it certainly separates me from Him but He's not going to beat me over the head, complain, or take action to prevent me from sinning. He wants me to see my sin for what it is. He's patient. He loves me. Once I really grasp this, changing my mistakes should become simple. In those realizations I will see another level of his goodness and run back to Him."

My wife, the love of my life, waited patiently for me to realize how wrong

I had been to be pursue another woman. Her patient endurance and her refusal to voice any objection became more convicting than any rebuke or complaint she could have levied. I was wrong, but it was is if she knew that my own realization of the error would have been more powerful than her words. I believe God's heart is much the same.

While at the time I was unable to correlate each dream with my life's circumstances, my perspective went through a refining process as I continued through the duration of that season. Looking back, I can see now that God wanted to reveal to me the presence and severity of my cancer (dream five) while also making it clear that it would take a special kind of treatment to combat it. He was also revealing his level of patience and his willingness to wait for me to come to the realization that my sin was affecting him and our relationship. And honestly that level of patience, grace and perseverance is so much more convicting than any tongue lashing or rebuke. It was that kind of treatment that would help me address my cancer.

And here's the truth of the matter: My cancer, my common form of cancer, the thing that is impervious to radiation and chemo and that ultimately could take me out — it's a subtle but very deeply rooted love of money.

I grew up on a 40-acre equestrian/hobby farm with two working parents who had tremendous love for my two sisters and me. It was a fantastic environment for any kid! My mom was a CPA and financial controller for a large specialty glass manufacturer and my father started a small software replication business before the internet was a thing. As I grew through middle school, my parent's financial success grew as well. In my teenage years, my sisters and I attended a prestigious private high school and we (our family) were taking multiple vacations each year to far off tropical destinations during the breaks in our schooling. In an attempt to build a good credit score, my parents gave me a credit card (for gas) that ended up being used on pretty much anything I wanted, with few questions ever raised. (I do not recommend this to any parent, **ever!**) Any time I needed cash for food my mom would flip me $20, which happened approximately 1-2 times per week.

On my 16th birthday I immediately had a nice car to drive and by 17

I was behind the wheel of a beautiful 2-year-old truck... a 1997 black V8 Dodge Dakota with an extended cab, a bed liner, 4WD, chrome wheels and a fantastic sound system.

Now, as hard as it may be to believe, I wasn't a spoiled brat. But I **was** incredibly spoiled. Unfortunately, I just didn't know it. Many of my peers at school were driving brand new cars (many of them German made), wearing designer clothing, and living in incredible homes in the west hills of Portland. Regardless of that comparison, my parents did the best they could, and I believe we were well behaved, good natured kids. Despite all that, I began to expect a certain standard of living and I believe it was in these formative years where my life became the perfect environment for this cancer to take root.

God waits patiently for us to come to our own revelation about our sin. (See 2 Peter 3:9 for reference) He's not going to demand our change, that would undermine the freedom he's provided us to choose. But **if** we choose him, we are certainly going to change. It's in our choosing him that we begin to understand the depth of his love and goodness — and that kind of love can only lead to a desire to change (repent) all the more. God's love becomes our **inspiration for choosing what's right** rather than the dangling carrot we are racing to catch, the **reward for doing what's right.** (Hopefully that analogy makes sense.)

But the effects of our choices, good or bad, have differing levels of consequence. For the sake of this chapter, I will speak to the negative side. Some of the consequences of our sin are immediate. For example, maybe you know someone who has gotten angry and decided to punch a wall only to end up with a broken hand. Hopefully that person considers a better outlet for their anger based on the immediate consequence of that stupid decision.

Other sin has impact that trails on for years, decades, even generations — a broken home for example. The consequences and fallout of divorce will often affect the lives of more than those divorcing. And while we know that God doesn't like our sin, in fact he detests it, I've come to see that he also won't force us away from it, even while we do our best to follow Jesus. And if he doesn't force us away from it, we will still feel the impact of whatever sin in which we engage.

Allow me to clarify here: Jesus' blood removes our sin but that doesn't mean that we won't feel the impact of ongoing sin in our lives.

If we choose to drink ourselves into a stupor, we will still experience the fallout of a hangover. Or if we open ourselves up to intimacy with someone, we also open ourselves up to any number of sexually transmitted diseases that person may carry. But God's love goes deep enough that he's willing to endure the hurt we inflict through our disobedience as we pursue other forms of fulfillment (idolatry). The realization of that grace is convicting! It's life changing! So much so that when our eyes are opened to our own blatant behavioral sin, we can't help but be overwhelmed by God's patience and his endurance; his waiting for us to realize it. And that realization should and usually does lead to lasting change!

Remember though, we can't always see the mess in which we're walking. From these two dreams it seemed like God was showing me that there was a cancerous infection deep inside me and its presence caused him significant pain. The more I thought through the entire dream series, the more I realized that the dreams were all connected. This sickness that had been identified, this subtle but deep affection for money was related to the four pillars of the dam in the river dream (Discontentment, Fear, Anxiety, and Expectations). But at the time, I still wasn't able connect the dots associating the four pillars to their bedrock — the love of money.

In reviewing my mindset shift to address discontentment (the first pillar) in my life, I had been mildly successful, but it was a temporary resolution at best. From time to time I found myself longing to be back on a farm, in a bigger home, in an overall better setting. But where had these desires come from?

Why was I not content with a small rental payment, living in close quarters with a family I love, a large yard, short commutes to work, grocery stores or entertainment within minutes from our home?

There were so many blessings in the life I was living and yet discontentment still crept in, even while attempting to fight it. I knew ten years in the future I'd be looking back at this time thinking how amazing it was… So why wasn't I able to appreciate it in the present? Maybe it stemmed from an inability to afford the place I really wanted and in that case, money played a significant role.

Adding to the complexity, my business was flourishing. In the six year history of the company, my income had always been steady and far greater than I had ever envisioned in year one, but it was a business where clients come and go and my competition had increased dramatically since its inception. Because of the client rotation and competition in the marketplace, anxiety about what the next month would bring was common and really centered around an imagined loss —

What if my clients fire me? What if my equipment breaks? What if the market falls off? In reality, my clients appreciate(d) me and my work. But the revenue never felt like it was enough. I wanted to provide more for my family.

In this imaginary fear of loss and the ensuing anxiety, money again played a significant role.

Going deeper on that line of thinking, I started comparing the life of my children to my life as a boy (I had it WAY better than my kids do now; or so I thought). Then, I compared myself to my parents to evaluate if I was better off than they were at my age. The same line of thinking followed with my peers, old high school friends, college friends, etc. I wanted to be more successful than all of them and my expectations were that I would surpass them in one way or another. Even worse, I always had to find an edge. I always had to "one up" my peers as I mentally compared our respective life circumstances. Once I found that advantage, I clung to it as a lifeline, a boost, an ace in the hole for my comparison. Nine times out of ten the advantage centered around money:

"I bet they don't make X. And even if they make X, I bet they don't have as much free time as me… Oh man, they drive what? I bet they're in debt up to their eyeballs."

All the criteria for evaluation and success involved financial comparisons.

It was an ugly reality, but it stemmed from an internal battle of ineptitude and insecurity. Unknowingly, I had placed unrealistic expectations on myself as I compared my life with those around me... and it all came back around to money.

I don't share all this junk to boast in it or to overly self-deprecate. I share it to reinforce the notion that we can't always see our own mess. God's revival never happens while we sit in our mess. It happens when something drastically changes. It happens when we catch a glimpse of the overwhelming love Father God has for each of us.

Looking back, I was in a sad state of life, but it was the honest truth of my heart condition at the time; the truth of my cancer. It had been growing and spreading in my life for decades; ever in the shadows, never drawing attention to itself. I was unaware of its presence: subtle and deeply rooted. The Lord was incredibly patient with me while I pursued this other love, while I worshiped this idol. Money, Mammon, this cancerous growth was at the root of my sin. Though I would never have admitted to it, I thought that perhaps having more money would alleviate my discontentment, my fear, my anxiety, and the expectations I had placed on my life. It was absolutely intertwined with the four pillars, killing all the Spirit life within me. It was my mistress. It had to go.

It's remarkable how God is able to use our individual circumstances in the natural to bring fresh revelation to our spirit, to our faith. Typically, these circumstances are intertwined with the most challenging seasons of our lives; the ones we will remember for decades.

And yet, it's within these challenging seasons that God is able to surgically remove our individual cancers and resuscitate every facet of our life. If you've not yet experienced this kind of season, you will one day. But take heart, this kind of hardship is evidence of God's love for you. At least that's what I told myself the day our hardship began.

CHAPTER 9

"THE ACCIDENT"

09

CHAPTER 9 — "THE ACCIDENT"

There were three missed calls and the text said, "URGENT! Please call!"

Receiving three missed calls from my wife was surprising enough. She rarely calls during the day and when she does, she typically won't leave a message, knowing she'll see me later or I'll call her back. But she had never sent a text like this one.

When I called her that morning, I didn't know what to expect. My mind raced. When she answered, she was clearly shaken but she had always been able to maintain composure. "Babe, I was in an accident. I need you here now."

My sleep (and subsequent mornings) became more peaceful as the dreams subsided. After selling our farm in September of 2017, we moved into our temporary rental in the middle of suburbia but we quickly missed the farm lifestyle. We helped some friends launch a farming co-op and began volunteering on a nearby dairy farm 45 minutes from our new home. In exchange for all the raw milk we could consume, I helped milk 2-3 cows once or twice a month.

Milking cows is actually a pretty demanding process. It was the end of Spring and the grass was exploding out of the ground. To say the cows lacked motivation to follow a stranger out of the fields and into the barn would be an another understatement.

Fortunately, the farm owners had equipped me with a secret weapon that made the ladies swoon… red clover hay. Once they realized the chocolate I was waving in front of them, the trouble transitioned from getting them to follow me to preventing them from trampling me.

But once I got them into the barn, the process of milking kicks off: Tie them up, clean the utters, connect the milking machine, give them hay, process the milk, turn them out, feed the pigs (that's a side job), and deep clean all the milk equipment. The whole process takes roughly 60-90 minutes depending upon the number of cows and how full they are. It was work, but so much more enjoyable than "sitting behind a desk" kind of work.

One particular Friday morning in May, my son Caleb and I went to the farm to double team the chores. I left my phone in the car while we did our work and it again was another typical glorious morning on the farm. Blue sky, sun rising, dew on the grass, birds chirping. Quiet. Calm. Peaceful. My favorite place to be at my favorite time of day. We had started our drive back to towards home when I looked at the phone and saw the barrage from Lauren.

She had hit someone. But that wasn't enough information. "Is everyone okay? Are you okay?" I asked later on the phone.

"No." She replied. "The police are here and the person I hit just left in an ambulance. Please meet me at the house as soon as you can."

She was scared — I could hear it. I was scared — I hoped she couldn't. "I'll be there as soon as I can."

I hung up the phone and called my folks who live nearby. "Mom, Lauren's been in an accident. I don't have all the info and I can't explain everything now, but I need you to meet me and take Caleb to school."

My mom and I have a good relationship. It's not amazing but it's not bad. It's been improving over the last few years. In our immediate family of five, we're very similar to one another... and she's really stubborn. Read into that all you'd like. So naturally, she and I were the only two in our family who never feared going toe to toe in an argument.

Love was something we could never break and we leaned hard on that belief. In regards to my mom, there were many things about which we disagreed while living under the same roof BUT one of the things I love about her is that whenever I combined the "This is Serious" voice with a call for help, she dropped everything to be there. I will always love her for that.

She picked up Caleb and I raced home.

When I arrived, Lauren was alone on the couch in our living room with a blanket over her lap. She stared out the window to our back yard with a glazed look on her face. Her eyes were bloodshot and puffy and her cheeks were still wet with fresh tears. It took a few moments of sitting with her before she was able to divulge what had transpired that morning.

I'll do my best to set the scene… In the rush to finish the farm chores and get all the kids to school, I had asked Lauren to take our two youngest to daycare. It was a cool morning and dew had accumulated on the windows of our family car — a 2008 Chevy Avalanche. I love our truck, but it has its flaws; one of which is larger than normal blind spots from the driver's seat.

Lauren's commute usually required her to turn right onto a major street outside our neighborhood each morning to get to work. But this morning, to drop the kids off, she had to turn left. (She's not Zoolander… she can turn left. She's actually a great driver.) But that morning, as she pulled into the intersection, she had a green light accompanied by a 'left turn yield to oncoming traffic' indicator.

As she slowly pulled into the intersection, she saw traffic approaching a long way off and decided she had plenty of time to make the turn. The distance she had coasted into the intersection allowed her to transition from looking straight ahead at oncoming traffic to looking out her driver side window in order to complete the turn. Unfortunately, in the time it took for her to pause in the intersection, a man had walked into the crosswalk, right into her blind spot.

Lauren wasn't on the phone, she wasn't changing a station on the stereo, and the kids weren't screaming in the backseat. There were no distractions. She just didn't see him. As she turned left, she didn't realize Charles was there until she had hit him.

She slammed on her breaks, jumped out of the car, and told someone who stopped to call 911. She then began administering first aid until help arrived.

Here is where I wish I could say… "and then I woke up." But this wasn't a dream.

Charles worked at a local grocery store for more than 20 years and was on his way to work that morning. He had Down Syndrome and lived with his mother and sister in an apartment not far from our home. I heard he was a fun-loving guy who many people in the community knew and appreciated. But I never got a chance to meet Charles.

What was God doing?

I remember her prayer that morning as she wept with me on the couch. "God, if he can't make a full and miraculous recovery, please have mercy and take him."

God was gracious.

I also remember her surrender in the week after the accident. While the police began their investigation, she shared with me that maybe God needed a light in the prison system. With that in mind, we mentally prepared for the worst-case scenario, uncertain if criminal charges would be filed. My close friend and family attorney informed us that it was a tragic accident and that we would be fine. Despite his confidence, our concern remained.

But what was God doing??

We asked the police if we could reach out to Charles' mother. We wanted to visit them at the hospital in the days following the accident. She did not express an openness to the visit but she did share her address. Somehow the flowers and sorrowful, heartfelt condolences and relay of prayers felt flat, unworthy. A mother was grieving her son and hoping for a miracle. Lauren was at fault and her position also brought with it a tremendous amount of loss.

So what was God doing???

I sent out a prayer request to a group of people at church the day of the accident. To say it was a challenging time does not paint the proper picture. My wife was in the ashy dust of anguish and there was nothing I could do to alleviate the pain.

The Sunday following the accident was a heavy day. Many tears flowed that morning. She continued managing the onslaught of emotion and I continued to support as best I could. As we worshiped my mind drifted from the accident to Charles' family, to our future, to his future.

We were interrupted during our worship that morning as a woman approached Lauren. She stood before her and very deliberately pulled a container of cream out of her pocket. When she opened it, I realized it wasn't cream, it was oil. Praying in the Spirit, she rubbed oil on Lauren's forehead, her throat, her chest and her palms. Then to my surprise she repeated the anointing on me.

We stood there in worship — anointed, breaking, crying, praying, and pleading for a miracle.

Charles passed away two days later. The head trauma he had received in the accident was too severe and the doctors, certain of catastrophic brain damage advised pulling life support. He died on a Tuesday morning. My wife had killed someone. She felt condemned, guilty, weighed down, confused, sad, scared and a myriad of other emotions far too complex to describe.

WHAT ARE YOU DOING GOD!?

From time to time we all hit rough patches in life. Rarely do we encounter circumstances that run overwhelmingly out of control but we had just entered one of those seasons. While I don't have experience living through one of these times without faith, I'm absolutely confident that God's love is the only thing that helps us walk through each derailment with grace. However, in those moments we have a choice:

We can either choose to let him be our GPS or we can self-navigate and hope for the best. The trouble with self-navigation is that it's easy to lose direction, due either to a misunderstanding of the present location or the bearing of the desired destination. In the coming months we would be presented with countless opportunities to depend on the Lord for direction or to take control and self navigate.

Another serious problem faced in any time of derailment is managing our self-perception. It's easy to get wrapped up in the drama of our circumstance and revert to an inauthentic identity. The scriptures say that as followers of Jesus we become sons and daughters of God — a chosen people, a royal priesthood! (See 1 Peter 2: 9) It's challenging enough to manage that healthy perspective when times are good and God is our active GPS. But when we start making decisions without consulting Him first, the enemy can easily manipulate our thinking.

Then when we slip up in self navigation the accuser will introduce shame and guilt into the equation.

Within weeks of the accident, Lauren bumped into an old work acquaintance who immediately introduced her to a new employee as a 'hero'. At this, the enemy went to work.

For that to make sense, you need to understand that Lauren's testimony carries some diverse experiences. Five years ago, she was in a restaurant in Portland where a man collapsed from a heart attack. Rather than call 911, she told someone else to call while she cleared space and performed CPR (for 10-15 minutes), ultimately saving the man's life. She didn't stick around after he was taken to the hospital by ambulance and she left before anyone could ask her name. But word had gotten out on social media that weekend about an unknown, heroic angel who had saved the man.

A coworker who had seen the social media frenzy happened to be walking past Lauren's office and overheard her private conversation with a friend. He stopped, interrupted the conversation and shared the social media buzz. The family wanted to meet and thank her!

It was a great experience watching my wife meet the man she had saved. Then the story got out amongst the people at her work and HR wrote up a story about her that was later shared with the entire company (75k+ people).

So when Lauren ran into her friend, whom she hadn't seen in years, he introduced her to the new employee as a hero, the woman who had saved someone's life. It was true... she had. But the enemy was right there speaking in the midst of the praise, "Ah yes, but you've also taken a life." It too was true.

But how did God view Lauren in that moment?

Clinging to the knowledge of how God views you can be the differentiator between successfully navigating a crisis (with faith in Jesus) and metaphorically driving off a cliff. For when your identity is dependent upon how well you self-navigate, it can very easily be manipulated. Contrarily, when you understand your identity in Jesus and you walk your faith in obedience to His lordship, your grounded foundation allows you to disregard the guilt and shame that may otherwise steer you off course. In one crazy moment Lauren had saved a life. In another, she had ended one. So was she a hero or a killer? More importantly that what we think... What does God think?

God didn't view Lauren as a life saver or a life taker. He viewed her in those moments as he always had... as his princess, his daughter, the delight of his eye.

We screw things up... it's the perpetual human condition. But when we walk with Jesus, our actions don't determine our identity. This is why our faith in him is so important! It's not our actions that make us righteous, but his. It's not our blood that will rectify our messed up situation, it's his. He is the source of a restored position before our good father.

Despite our crazy circumstance, God was reminding us that he was as good in the moments of difficulty as he had ever been. Because of that, we trusted that whatever we walked through we were loved by him. That's not to say that we didn't struggle in the chaos.

Psalm 27 records a poem of David in which he cries out to the Lord for help. And yet even in the midst of his hardship he is able to remind himself of God's goodness. "I am still confident of this: I will see the goodness of the Lord in the land of the living. Wait for the Lord; be strong and take heart and wait for the Lord." (Psalm 27: 13-14)

God is our rock. The Alpha and the Omega. The Beginning and the End. He is the good shepherd and his rod and staff comfort us. He is righteous. He is Holy.

But what exactly was He doing?

CHAPTER 10

"DIRECT DOWNLOADS"

"No, that's totally normal. They just want to make sure you're not, like, Bill Gates and under insured. D'you know what I mean?"

"Well, what difference would that make?" I said with honest curiosity.

"Well, no, they just want to make sure you're not under insured but have, like, a second house or anything that could be sold."

"But what difference would that make?" I responded, now a bit perturbed.

"Well, no, I mean, they just want to make sure you're not driving really nice cars or something like that."

"BUT WHAT DIFFERENCE DOES THAT MAKE!?"

I couldn't believe what I was hearing. A claims specialist from our insurance provider had just informed me that a newly formed estate was requesting all of our financial information. They wanted to know exactly what we were worth. I was concerned something like this was coming but I did not expect to have the process ushered along by someone claiming to do everything in their power to protect our family.

We had made a massive mistake in our financial plan. While we carried auto insurance with liability coverage up to $100,000, we had dropped our $1MM umbrella policy after selling our farm. How likely was it that we'd ever get into an accident and cause more than $100,000 in damages, right? (If you do not have an umbrella policy, please allow our mistake to be your life lesson. For under $15/month you can cover your family for up to one million dollars if something catastrophic were to ever happen... and believe me, it can happen.)

Shortly after Charles' death, his mother (who was also mildly handicapped and had grown somewhat dependent upon Charles' income) hired an attorney and created an estate in his name. The attorney then issued an affidavit to our insurance company demanding financial information. I suppose I should say "politely requesting" rather than demanding. It would become much worse in the coming months.

How much do we make? How much do we have saved? How much is our home worth? How much equity do we have in it? How many cars do we drive and what are their values? How much is in our retirement accounts? Stock accounts?

They were planning on suing us to make restitution for their loss. I can understand their position but the whole process just felt slimy. Why was the value of his life dependent upon the total value of our assets? Adding to our hesitancy in responding was the fact that the affidavit came to us with absolutely zero formality. My eighth grade history worksheets looked more professional than this document. No heading, no cover letter, no introduction. Not only that, but there were grammatical and spelling errors. If someone hadn't died, I would have laughed it off and disregarded the whole thing.

But someone had died. And my claims specialist, who I'm sure received plenty of training prior to entering his position, sounded like a recent college graduate stuttering over his words when I pushed back on his Bill Gates comment.

"Do you trust me?"

The question hit me a few days after my conversation with the insurance company. I'd like to say I heard the voice as clearly as I could hear anyone in a conversation, but I'd be lying. Instead it was an overwhelming thought that echoed through my soul, a download that stopped me mid-stride. It was very matter of fact and I believe now that it was to be the theme of the ensuing months.

"Of course I trust you God. You're God! But what are you doing in all of this and what are we supposed to be doing?"

Crickets. Silence. Nothing.

I shared the experience with my wife. We prayed. We relinquished. Then we spoke with our attorney.

AJ (my attorney and close friend) casually advised me not to send any info about our financial well-being while we were walking down the fairway of a local golf course. But this was my first rodeo with death and lawsuits. His calm demeanor didn't match my own, nor did it rub off on me. We were scared, and his advice seemed flippant.

When the claims representative told me that this was all part of the process it still felt gross... they were fishing to see if we would become their cash cow. The more they knew, the closer they could get to a "reasonable" demand. What's more, the insurance company said that we were required to complete the information request within three weeks. They didn't elaborate on what would happen if we didn't complete it — they just said it was a requirement. And they were on our side... right?

(Please note that insurance companies do not take sides. The only thing they want is to pay out what is owed as quickly as possible. They're neutral. We paid for insurance covering $100,000 in total liability and they wanted to pay that amount and move on. However, we were potentially liable for upwards of $1.1-1.3 million.)

When they told us they were going to do everything in their power to protect us, that power was limited to the $100,000 payout they were obligated by law to pay. Beyond that, the company didn't care about Charles, his mother, or our family. That may be cold, but to them it was business, not life or death (for Charles' family) or financial depletion (for us).

David often writes about his enemies in the psalms — men pursuing him, eager to take his life. As we ventured further down the road of this season, we felt more and more attacked with every demand for information. For the first time ever, we felt like we had an enemy and the stink of it was that it had all come out of tragedy. Think about that... how many people can claim to have an enemy?

I don't mean an enemy of our country or an opponent we may have faced in a sporting event; I'm talking about an individual who's single pursuit is to berate you, wear you down, beat the tar out of you and then take your lunch money (or whatever they could get). A real enemy.

Our enemy wasn't Charles' family. For them we felt nothing but sadness and an honest desire to do what was right, though we weren't exactly sure what that meant. Was our enemy the attorney who stood to earn approximately 40% of whatever could be squeezed out of a judgment or settlement? It sure felt like it. We didn't think he saw us as a scared, grieving family. In us he saw dollar signs, or so we assumed. But we ran with that... in our fear and his persistence, we made the attorney out to be our enemy.

In the beginning we had reluctantly divulged information to him about a number of our financial assets. We even got so detailed as to list out our monthly budget for his review. In addition to AJ, we had an appointed attorney as part of our coverage. In conversation with her, she relayed that the estate attorney had flippantly commented to her, "How can your clients feel justified continuing to pay into their 401k when my client's son has been killed? And honestly, this food budget seems exorbitantly high for a small family."

Okay, first off, our food budget was artificially low due to the farming activities from our recent past. We had raised our own meat on the farm and still had two freezers full of it. Second, his comment about our retirement investing felt like a low blow. I was pissed. And sad. And defensive. It was a torrent of emotion, but we felt attacked.

Nearly every week we received a request for more information... paystubs, stock balances, bank statements, social security numbers. At one point he even had the audacity to demand the personal information of our three children.

The most frustrating part of the process was when he asked questions that had already been answered in the documentation we had previously submitted. Questions that could have easily been answered by a thorough review of the information in those documents.

"Dude! Do your homework! Read what we've already sent you. The answers are there. Good grief!"

It was aggravating. Every answered question led to three more unnecessary clarification questions. What they really wanted was validation of our net worth and as soon as we felt like we had exposed everything, more questions would be delivered.

"Do you trust me?"

We heard it repeatedly for weeks on end. It was the first of three words God would speak to us. But it was rhetorical… a reminder.

We knew of God's goodness. 'King of My Heart' by Bethel was one of our favorite songs. Not just for worship… it was one of our favorites in general. "Let the king of my heart be the fire inside my veins, the echo of my days, oh he is my song." It's powerful!

Now, take a step back with me for a minute. Charles' mother had lost her son in an accident. The police concluded that neither party was at fault and the district attorney had decided not to press charges. Lauren had hit him, and he later died from his injuries. His mother's most prudent action was to hire an attorney to help seek restitution that would cover medical bills associated with the accident and the loss of her son and his future income, savings, retirement, etc. — that all made sense. Any detached, third party observer would agree. She was a grieving mother loaded with a recent $160,000 medical bill. She was not our enemy.

The attorney she hired (we'll call just him Mark) had a moral obligation to pursue a judgment that would cover as much as he could legally prove his client was owed. Her financial future (again because she was somewhat dependent upon Charles) was in his hands. Forget about what Mark would collect out of the final amount; it was his job to fight for her. He fought and dug and wormed his way into every crevice of our finances. He was doing his job and he was very good at it. But he was not our enemy.

We knew we had a moral obligation to Charles' mother via his estate. We wanted to support her but how much was enough? Were we expected to sacrifice our financial well-being and livelihood indefinitely?

How do you value a life? Charles' life? And could we pay that sum? If we looked at ourselves through the eyes of Charles' mother, we were the careless drivers who hit her son as he legally crossed an intersection en route to work. Who were we to resist questioning? Were we their enemy?

"Do you trust me?" God had asked.

After months of back and forth questioning, we realized there weren't any good guys or bad guys in this story. There was no enemy. There was only tragedy. So why did it feel like we had an enemy? How were the spiritual powers playing into this?

"Jesus, we trust you. Holy Spirit, we trust you. God, we trust you. Father, what would you have us do?"

"Reveal Everything."

Come again!?

In light of the ongoing demands, this word from Holy Spirit felt like we were being asked to open our play book, make photo copies of our game plan and hand it to the opposing team. If they knew everything, they would want everything. For example:

Q: When did you buy your current home?
A: After the accident — Hmmm... This made it look like we were trying to hide assets. We weren't... we had been house shopping for some time by then and had been under contract on two homes prior to the accident. But you can see how that may appear to an attorney whose job is to investigate and assess the financial wellbeing of an opposing party. It led to an additional 2-3 rounds of questioning.

Q: Have you received a raise or made any adjustments to your retirement investing since the accident?
A: DANG IT! Yes. Lauren had just gotten a raise three months after the questioning began and it allowed us to turn her retirement savings back up to the Dave Ramsey recommended 15%. I really didn't want to share about the raise. That question also revealed that Lauren began making more money after the accident. Mark would assume that she could then afford to pay more.

Lauren knew I would hesitate in answering the questions about her recent raise, so when we were both included on an email asking if there had been any recent compensation increases, she answered before we could discuss.

Our obedience to Jesus' call to **"Reveal Everything"** definitely would have tested my resolve. But obedience with a partner made it easier to proceed...

mostly because when one of us was weak (not wanting to fully submit) the other would move forward in obedience. We had both been given that second word from the Lord and we were resolved about sharing any information they requested... despite our occasional kicking and screaming.

The more he dug for info, the more Mark thought he smelled a rat. I wanted AJ (my friend and attorney) to "go to bat" for us but he refused with sound reasoning — hiring additional counsel would highlight that we had funds available to fight, which would make the opposing counsel even more aggressive.

Instead he advised we hire a bankruptcy attorney. His logic was remarkable:

A bankruptcy attorney would help us formally prepare our financial documentation in a way that an attorney and a judge (if it went that far) would understand. More importantly, it subtly sent the message that bankruptcy was an option. The estate would receive little to nothing if we filed so we went through the entire bankruptcy process and stopped just short of hitting "Submit."

That process in itself made me feel exposed and bled out. The work that goes into preparing bankruptcy documentation is a draining process of questioning and document collection. We bared our financial souls. Every spare nickel was out there for review and all the supporting documentation was there to prove it. I even shared about our untraceable assets - gold and silver coins along with a significant amount of cash we kept on hand in case of an emergency.

We submitted the paperwork (our financial DNA) and felt like our obedience added some personal substance to the monetary proclamation "In God We Trust."

Shortly thereafter we attended a Friday night worship session at the church and I received yet another word from Holy Spirit. Forget the dreams, I was now receiving direct downloads, and it was about to get exponentially more difficult.

God: Do you trust me?
M&L: Yes Sir!

God: Reveal Everything.
M&L: Affirmative.

God: Don't Fight.
M&L: Wait... What!?

87

"OBEDIENCE"

CHAPTER 11 — "OBEDIENCE"

Don't fight? — Don't fight!?

God, how is that possible in the midst of a mediation?

In the book of Exodus, Moses leads the people of Israel out of Egypt after God decimates the country with plagues. In the mass migration away from their task masters, the people walked away from a land filled with plentiful harvests and into a dessert led by a man whom they barely knew. I'm sure faith was involved in this one.

One of the suspected routes took an estimated one million people east out of Egypt and then south along the western coastline of the Sinai Peninsula. Eventually they rounded the southern point but as they turned north, that mass of people was confronted by a mountain range of impassible terrain that ran into the Red Sea, today's modern-day Gulf of Adaba. (Do a Google Map search on this one and you can get an idea of the topography.)

One million people were hemmed in. Mountains to the north and west and a massive body of water to the east. The only way to move was to head back the way they had come, which is exactly what God told Moses to do.

In the midst of this, Pharaoh had changed his mind, rallied his troops and set out in hot pursuit. As God's people turned back, following the direction from the Lord through Moses, the Egyptians made their way around the tip of the peninsula and came into view. The might of Egypt was bearing down on them and the tremendous loss experienced by the Egyptians would be avenged with spilt blood in the desert.

Terror struck the camp. Many would be slaughtered; the rest would be marched back to their lives of servitude. What could they do? Running wasn't an option — not for a mass of people that size. Would they fight? They had no weapons! They were stuck. God had placed them in what seemed like an impossible position.

In their distress they wailed against Moses. (I never understood this though. God had just delivered them from Egypt on the heels of 10 impossible plagues and rather than cry out to God, they cried out in complaint against Moses). "Was it because there were no graves in Egypt that you brought us out to the desert to die!?" (Exodus 14:11)

Moses (Aaron with him) replies to the people, "Do not be afraid. Stand firm and you will see the deliverance the Lord will bring you today. The Egyptians you see today you will never see again. **The Lord will fight for you; you need only to be still."** (Exodus 14: 11-14)

Don't Fight.

The Holy Spirit had spoken these words to my heart along with the Exodus scripture reference during a worship conference in November and I knew in my spirit that I was supposed to share it with the entire group. Unplanned and unrehearsed, I walked onto the stage and in tears looked at my wife. "We're not supposed to fight it babe."

I then laid out the fear experienced by the Israelites, internally referencing and harnessing my own fear to add emphasis to the message God was communicating to others in the audience. The Israelites were told to be still; God would fight for them. That would require them to trust Him completely. There was no room for fear in their camp. There was no room for fear in that audience. There was no room for fear in my (our) heart(s). We trusted the Lord.

'Don't fight' was the message we had received and the scripture to support it emphasized that God would take care of the fighting.

Both scenarios (Israel v. Egypt and Hammonds v. The Estate) were ridiculous. The Israelites were tasked with patiently waiting for God to intercede while staring down the advance of their attackers. We were to walk into a mediation without plans to protect ourselves, our children, our future. It didn't make sense. But if it did, would we really need to trust the Lord?

I believe God appreciates when we ask questions. Not in a demanding interrogation sort of way, but he's looking for us to ask questions that when answered will draw us closer to him. Without asking our questions of God, it makes it very difficult build trust. And you'll never truly surrender to God without that trust.

More importantly, without surrender, your faith cannot take root. And I'm not just talking about "Jesus take the wheel" kind of faith. I'm talking about surrendering to the cleansing power of Holy Spirit as he clears out the junk from our past.

Personally, I had been fighting on my own for so long that it no longer felt like fighting. Nor did I realize that I was alone in the fight. It was just a normal part of everyday life. Buttoning things up had become the "status quo" and I knew that everyone else, just like me, was facing the same battles surrounding money, fear, and expectations amongst other things.

But intimacy with Jesus, a true connecting, is completely dependent upon our surrender.

We can't hold back any area of our heart and expect God to take possession of it. He's going to be the one who restores you by taking you back to your deepest hurts, cleansing your wounds, and healing them with an intense and comforting love. Until we provide access, he patiently waits on us and answers our questions.

And God will answer when you cry out with your questions!!

But God will also show up when we cry out in surrender... "The Lord will fight for you; you need only to be still." (Exodus 14:14) If there is any encouragement that can be taken at this point in the story, I would say drop your guard, drop your defenses. Ask God your questions, allow him to work, and his response will be more than just an emotional blip on your spiritual radar. It will astound you!

By this time in our story, I was out of new questions to ask! My questioning of the circumstance and God's plan was on a never ending repeat. It was getting old even though he was providing us an occasional word of encouragement.

We had just received our third message from the Lord. Six days later, we received a demand for more information from the estate attorney that nearly put us over the edge. I can't remember the exact request or the tone in which it was delivered, but Lauren was so distraught, so angry after reading the note that she stepped away from her desk and locked herself in a private office for nearly three hours to scream, argue, pray, and wrestle with God.

Why God!? WHY!?

Thoughts raced through my mind. More than anything we wanted to say "Screw it! Take us to court, we're not paying you a dime!" We had already completed the footwork for the bankruptcy. If they filed the suit and received a substantial judgment, we'd pull the trigger and actually process the bankruptcy paperwork.

As a second wave of defense, if they decided to garnish wages after the bankruptcy, Lauren would just quit working so there wouldn't be any wages to garnish. They'd be left with nothing. It was our nuclear option and we were ready to press the red button. But I knew that was not the direction the Lord was leading.

I wish I could remember how ridiculous the request had been, but it was a stretch, a "Hail Mary." It was their last attempt to rattle us, hoping we would slip up and divulge anything beyond what we had already shared. In my distress I prayed. Then I wrestled and yelled at God. I thought briefly about punching a wall... but I settled for calling AJ.

"Dude, he keeps asking for the same things repeatedly after we've already provided them! Then he demands that we jump through all these additional hoops and the threats that follow are almost as ridiculous as the demands! What in the world are we supposed to do!?" I asked.

"Matt, you gotta settle down. He's lobbing bombs just to rattle you. Think of it like this: your mediation is going to be a boxing match (ironic in light of the word we had received). It's how every mediation goes. It's a back and forth dance of jabs and blocks with a mediator delivering each blow. If he can land body blows before you even show up, you'll go in bloody and bruised, in no condition to fight. You'll only be thinking only about the coming relief and be happy to accept a higher number just to end the abuse!"

AJ's words were **gold**, and I knew the wisdom he had provided was a gift from the Lord. He **WAS** answering our questions.

As previously mentioned, Mark (the estate attorney) wasn't our enemy. He was doing his job, seeking restitution for the loss of his client. Every request he had made was designed to make us uncomfortable. Every threat carried the intention of making us consider the worst-case scenario. The demands were presented repeatedly to weigh us down with the burden of collecting more documentation; disrupting our life to make us long for relief. In case I've not emphasized it enough, Mark was **really** good at his job.

Don't Fight.

That was the word and after AJ's insight, we changed our perspective on the demands for information:

> "Consider it pure joy my brothers, whenever you face trials of many kinds because you know that the testing of your faith develops perseverance. Perseverance must finish its work so that you may be mature, complete, not lacking anything." (James 1: 2-4)

It took some mental focus but from that point on, Lauren and I began looking at each request like an opportunity to clear our name. They suspected that we were hiding assets, income, anything of value and I suppose that would be the status quo of human nature. So, every time we got an info request, we forced ourselves to laugh at the audacity of it and trust that God really was in control.

Lauren forced herself to take pleasure in stepping away from work to collect 2-year-old paystubs or bank statements and I did the same when I had to retrieve random documentation about mortgages, car purchases, and other assets. We reminded each other of the boxing analogy and our 'Don't Fight' calling. We encouraged each other to stay faithful to God's word and the assumption that if he fought off Egypt for Israel, he could surely fight for us too.

The change in perspective allowed us to sidestep the jabs and body blows. Trusting that God would fight for us provided a means to shift our approach which in turn provided a clarity that allowed us to trust God even more! It was a positive cycle of reinforcement and while it stemmed from AJ's words of wisdom, trusting God had been the resounding theme of this season of life. It also happened to be the first direct word we heard from Holy Spirit for this period of our lives.

Trusting God (the first word from Holy Spirit) allowed us to reveal all the information needed to clear our name (the second word from Holy Spirit) and it gave us confidence that we didn't have to fight this battle (our third word). God would be there to support us through all of it if we would just trust His goodness.

And there-in lies a mission critical secret to walking closely with the Lord... the more you understand God's goodness, the more you will feel supported by him. As simple as it may sound, he loves you more than you know. Once you understand this concept, believe it, and cling to it in faith, it will radically change your approach to any hardship.

Side story: I tell my kids that I love them every chance I get, but especially when I step away for a prolonged period of time. I'll usually get a response in kind but every now and then they'll respond with 'I love you more.'

"I'm not sure that's possible," I say back and chuckle at the thought. It's cute, but seriously, it's preposterous. The depth of love I have for my kids, the depth of love you have (or will have) for yours... there's just no way they could EVER love us the same way and they couldn't possibly understand it... Right?

So what makes us think we could possibly understand the depths of God's love for his children? His good creation? For you!

In my case, the Holy Spirit wanted to cure me of a cancerous growth stemming from a deep-rooted love of money. He used dreams to reveal that I had shaken hands with discontentment, fear, anxiety and ridiculous expectations that had subconsciously altered the way I viewed myself before the Lord. Even more, my thoughts had unknowingly made me insecure about the depths of his love for me, which made it harder to trust him. This subconscious negative spiral killed every bit of spirit filled life that I was meant to enjoy with Father God.

Despite all that, God's love for me (and for you) never wavered. Before we were in the womb, he knew us completely! (Psalm 139: 13-16) Even when we're in the midst of horrible mistakes (sin), his great love had already sent Jesus to the cross so that we might have a chance to come to a realization of his love. He is SO GOOD!

Here's the thing, the more you comprehend the goodness of God's love, (though we'll never understand the depths of it completely), the more you will be emboldened with a new wisdom, a new knowledge that will enable a perspective shift in any circumstance.

Even reminding yourself that his love is never ending, that it's not dependent upon you whatsoever, will allow you to trust him more completely. And just like we experienced, the mindset shift will make you all the more grateful for his love within your circumstance! It's an amazing upward spiral of hope!

Despite our commitment to abstain from fighting (before, during or after the mediation) we decided to retain the services of both attorneys for the mediation, one being paid by our insurance company and the other out of pocket (our bankruptcy attorney). Their presence would allow us to ask clarifying questions and would make communication with the mediator (a retired judge) a bit more fluid than if we were on our own.

We still had no idea what to expect walking into a mediation without the intent to fight, but we trusted God to step in.

If I said that this page of our lives was turning slower than Christmas, I would be telling the truth because the mediation was delayed from October 2018 to February of 2019. I was really hoping to close this chapter of our lives before 2018 concluded but apparently that would not be the case. Furthermore, despite our understanding of God's love and the newly found optimism to which we clung, I'd be lying if I said there wasn't a mental cloud of foreboding in the recesses of my mind every morning when I awoke.

More than anything it felt like life was on hold. Leading up to the settlement it was as if we were "going through the motions" of life. We couldn't plan anything for our future until things were settled. That cloud was present through the holiday season and stayed with us until early February when yet again, we received another word from the Lord. But this time it was different. This time it wasn't a challenge or directive. This time there was hope.

"STRETCHING US"

12

CHAPTER 12 — "STRETCHING US"

For 15 years I had attempted to restrict God's Holy Spirit from accessing my life, and for 15 years my faith had been just a flicker of the raging inferno God intended it to be. That's not to say that there were no victories and that Jesus was not present in that time. I knew the Lord was with me but I was as blind to my very deep character sins as the addict is to their own.

God's grace and his patience are incredible! The amazing thing is that despite my attempt to quarantine Holy Spirit, the scriptures are pretty clear that this is impossible. One passage in particular caught my attention. As Paul is talking about the gifts of the Holy Spirit he says, "All these are the work of one and the same Spirit, and he distributes them to each one, just as he determines." (1 Corinthians 12: 11)

I love this! The Holy Spirit determines the who, what, where, why and when of the outpouring. He gives us the gifts, but he also works out the details. So then, the question I would pose to the old me (the one who was uncomfortable with anything involving Holy Spirit) and others like him is this: Do you really think you are capable of holding back God's Holy Spirit? Or could it be that the logic loving side of your brain isn't capable of processing all that goes with the outpouring of His amazing power?

Back to the story...

In my imagination, mediation was held in a boardroom with a long, fancy table stretching the length of the room surrounded by multiple high-backed chairs and a view that stretched out to the horizon. An imposing board room. The two parties come together from doors on opposite sides of the room (the table between them) and the respective attorneys would argue back and forth, countering and re-countering the other's position. Again, in my imagination, this would continue until either the parties agree to terms or one gets frustrated and storms out declaring, "I'll see you in court!"

In reality, mediation is a double-blind, back and forth game of waiting, shock, indignation, strategy, and counteroffers.

In our case, both parties were on the same floor but in different offices of a high rise in downtown Portland. Our mediator, a sweet (but fierce) retired judge traveled back and forth between two rooms relaying messages and offers. Neither side really wanted to be there, and it was the mediator's job to get each side uncomfortable with their position so each would be willing to take steps to meet the opposing party somewhere in the middle.

Lauren and I sat in our meeting room, which did happen to have a great view of downtown Portland, with our two confidants (our bankruptcy and insurance appointed attorneys). We had done a **rough estimate** of our net worth and knew we had a little more than $100,000 in relatively liquid assets. The other side had a pretty good idea of this figure as well. What they didn't know was that we were no longer fighting for ourselves.

Flash back: Between May of 2018 and February of 2019, Lauren rode the roller coaster of emotions associated with the accident and ending someone's life — guilt and shame were her biggest accusers followed closely by regret and busyness (as a form of escape).

Despite the revelations Holy Spirit had provided about my dreams, I continued wrestling with my cancer and the damn dam. Ongoing discontentment with our circumstance and the expectations of an imagined trajectory of our lives weighed heavily on my mind. Fear and anxiety ran wild with the uncertainty of our coming appointment and seemed to compound knowing we would be paying out a significant sum.

The constant unknowns were the biggest waste of time, but they often got the better of me (Lauren too, but less so) as we waited. There were times where we just sat together at home on the couch... processing, feeling the weight of what happened and wondering about what was coming. Despite all the setbacks and continued wrestling, we were healing. In hindsight, we needed that time to be still. (Sometimes I hate hindsight.) As much as we would have liked to fast forward through those months, it was to our own benefit they moved as quickly as a continental plate.

We were two weeks out from our mediation and church had just wrapped up that Sunday morning. After packing up our things, a friend familiar with our pending appointment approached Lauren with some encouragement.

When Lauren talked to me later in the day she had a different countenance about her. Lauren was lighter, she was smiling. The woman had shared her excitement about what we were about to go through, that we would approach the settlement as an offering to the Lord rather than an obligation of debt. At that suggestion, something clicked in Lauren's mind and heart. It was as if scales fell from her eyes and she could see (in the Spirit) the amazing opportunity in the coming meeting. When she relayed the message to me, the same thing happened.

This was going to be an offering! We were going to give everything we could to Charles' mother as an act of worship, not out of obligation — and we knew we had to give our absolute best, holding nothing back!

If the settlement came in less than the liquid assets we had on hand, the remainder of what we had would go to Charles' mother directly... a gift we would send after everything had settled. Contrarily, if the number came in higher, we knew God would provide a way to stand up under it. Either way, we were giving everything we had and we weren't fighting the estate. If we were fighting at all, it was to keep money out of the hands of her attorney so it would end up going to her directly... We were on the same team and we would be giving our very best.

By that point we were nearly through the throes of a fabulous waiting game (nearly nine months since the accident) and FINALLY, with that newfound direction, a peace settled over us that could only be described as miraculous. I don't think it arose because we could see light at the end of the insanely long tunnel, though that certainly helped. We were at peace because we felt like God had provided us with a GPS location and a heading. We had our game plan and it aligned with what the Lord had intended, the words he had given us. We trusted him. We had revealed everything. We would not be fighting.

The meeting kicked off at 10:30 on a Tuesday morning with a $635k disparity. By 4:45 that afternoon, the difference had dropped to $20k. In other words, the negotiations started at $650k (their initial offer) and $15k (our initial offer) and near the end line we were down to $120k (their demand) and $100k (our offer). In fact, we had just relayed to them that all we had was a bit more than $100k and we truly couldn't afford to go any higher.

This was not a tactic to win them over, we really didn't think we had anything more to offer. It was $100,000 for crying out loud! I know that's chump change to some and to others its more than they can imagine, but that's more money than I've ever dealt with. It had taken us years to save this much. It was heavy! And knowing they were demanding more was hard to comprehend. But they didn't budge, they wanted $120,000 and the settlement was ours to accept or decline.

I couldn't help wondering if they wanted us to suffer as retribution... did they care that we were a young family just trying to make it? An ongoing monthly payment was something I was adamantly opposed to before our mediation began. It was off the table. Period. I didn't want to be reminded every month that we were being financially crippled because of a horrible accident. Nor did I want the feeling of despair that would accompany it.

But here we were, facing a payout of a huge sum of money, some of which we didn't have. We could either agree to the amount and be forced into payments totaling $20k, or we could refuse and call off the meeting. The implications of calling it off were also a bit daunting... it would mean depositions where Lauren and Charles' mother would have to retell their respective sides of the story, both would relive the experience and answer to barrage of questioning. It would mean ongoing legal fees, a judge/jury declaring how much we owed, a potential bankruptcy... it just didn't fit right, especially in light of the specific words we had received from the Lord. Neither option felt good.

In the end, we decided to accept their offer. The total we would owe would be $119,500. Neither party had won but we certainly felt conflicted: The months of interrogation were now over and the questions about our future had been answered. We could turn the page and move forward and we hoped Charles' family could do the same. We just had to figure out how to raise $20k in a rather short window of time.

When we arrived home that evening, I pulled out the computer and began tallying the accounts. Again, we hadn't done a formal audit prior to the mediation and it had been a few months since we had finalized the bankruptcy documentation. We knew we had approximately 100k in relatively liquid assets. Here was the approximate breakout:

$26k - Gold & Silver Coins
$10k - Cash on hand
$54k - Employee Stock
$30k - Cash in savings

Tally that up... did you catch it?

That total came to $120, not $100. **ONE HUNDRED TWENTY NOT ONE HUNDRED!!!** How could I have missed this? I'm a numbers guy and a recovering financial addict. How could I have not performed and audit beforehand and known this figure!? We were free!

Had the legal system been able to process things faster, we could have written a check immediately! How was this possible!? Our total asset count was literally within a few hundred dollars of the final settlement.

Immediately I knew in my spirit that God had been stretching us. Would we trust him through the interrogation and the heat of the mediation? Would we reveal everything when asked? Would we fight? He had asked his questions, provided his counsel and guided us through the valley, all the while listening to our own incessant line of questioning. We were done and to our surprise, we had EXACTLY what was needed to move forward.

He had spoken. It was the most surreal moment of a very crazy day in the hardest season of our lives. As I thought back on the series of events and the potential correlation with my dreams, I got a sense that the pillars of the dam in my river dream began to loosen. I felt the cancerous bedrock holding them in place (my love of money) begin to crack.

"Throughout our history God has spoken to our ancestors by his prophets in many different ways. The revelation he gave them was only a fragment at a time, building one truth upon another. But to us living in these last days, God now speaks to us openly in the language of a

Son, the appointed Heir of everything, for through him God created the panorama of all things and all time." (Hebrews 1: 1-2)

Do you believe that? I mean really believe it? Do you really believe that God speaks directly to us as his sons and daughters? We know that God spoke to prophets of old who would then relay the message to His people - that's what makes up a good chunk of the Old Testament.

But just before Jesus left the earth, he said it would be better that he go away. Why? Because the one coming after him would be a better helper, a divine encourager.

But today it seems there's a disconnect with the communication medium; many who call themselves followers of Jesus refuse to acknowledge the gifts of the Holy Spirit he referenced. In my experience, the old me wasn't able to understand Holy Spirit so there was no way that I'd ever extend the invitation for a powwow... how would I discern between his voice and my own thoughts?

My lack of understanding and our collective inability to ever fully understand prevented my openness to this resource that Jesus touted so highly.

That said, even if we could wrap our heads around Holy Spirt, I don't believe we'd ever be able to fully comprehend the influence he wields, the medium through which he works, or the game plan he's established for this world. But does that really matter? And should our inability to comprehend prevent us from taking Jesus at his word?

I used to label people religious when hands were raised in worship... so praying in tongues, miraculous healing and prophecy wasn't even in the ballpark of reality. Anyone associated with "that kind of Christianity" was biblically unfounded, emotionally charged, and immature in the faith. My logic agreed with Jeremiah 17: 9... We will never fully understand the emotional wielding of the heart, so why would we ever fully trust our heart, let alone our thoughts? (I'm sure I bit into a bit of misinterpretation when I memorized that scripture.)

But didn't Jesus say he would send us a counselor, one who would teach us and guide us? The Holy Spirit does far more than live inside us when we submit to Jesus as Lord. He becomes that counselor. He speaks to us. To you and me.

I know that my ability to hear him can be stunted by the number of distractions I allow in my life — an LED screen keeps me up late and affects my sleep so I don't dream very often (it's often the first thing I reach for in the morning as well). My car stereo is always playing some kind of music or podcast. I'm constantly addressing the next item on the "To Do" list whenever I'm home. All of these factors (and more) add to the cacophony of life that makes it hard to hear from a God known for speaking in a gentle whisper.

Over the last two years I've found that listening for the Spirit is a critical component to actually hearing. And I know that may sound stupidly obvious but the reality of our culture is that we need a simplified version of this kind of truth. So... how badly do you want to hear from the Lord? Are you willing to rearrange your schedule to make space? And are you willing to begin flexing a muscle that for many of us, lays atrophied and dormant?

After we were stretched by the mediation, I was done trying to "logic" my way through life. God had been speaking to us directly and counseling us through the entire ordeal. We just had to tune our ears and create space for our spirits to hear.

For over 15 years I had been a logical, check the box follower of Jesus; I was sold out for Jesus (as best as I could be) and yet I always had trouble hearing from him. Not because I doubted that he spoke, (I knew he spoke) but my perspective on his interaction was only ever in hindsight, never in the present. I'd look back and say, "Wow God, I'm so grateful you worked that out!"

But now I understand that God/Jesus/Holy Spirit speaks to me in the present and can help guide me if I tune my ears and position myself to hear his voice. The same power is at your disposal as well. Holy Spirit wants to speak to you and have dialogue with you. He wants to give you insight and guidance on how to handle the complicated situations you face.

Holy Spirit posed the question, "Do you trust me?" He told us to reveal all of our financial documents to an aggressive attorney prior to a lawsuit... which didn't make any sense. THEN he told us not to fight before and during the mediation... which also didn't make sense. But as I look back on that season of our life, the steps we took to hear what the Holy Spirit had to say payed enormous dividends in hearing him clearly.

That same ability to hear His voice resides in you as well. And the most thrilling part about hearing His voice and stepping out in faith occurs when you receive a confirmation from a third party. It's a jaw-dropping, faith-building, "How in the world!?" kind of experience. It had recently happened through people's words, but our next confirmation came from a 2,000-year-old piece of metal.

> **That same ability to hear His voice resides in you as well.**

"THE EBENEZER"

CHAPTER 13 — "THE EBENEZER"

Gold and silver coins are not what I would call a solid financial investment. While my parents at one time or another had enjoyed a season of "prepping", I had mostly abstained from the hysteria that seemed to grip segments of our nation's populace over the last 10-15 years. That said, I was not immune to the conversations propagated by daytime radio advertisements, conservative talk show hosts, and yes, even my own parents' discussions of bean and rice stockpiling. Even the "normal" people of Portland were prepping, they just did it under the guise and laugh of a "Zombie Apocalypse."

Beginning around the year 2007, every birthday within my young family included a gift of silver coins from my parents, typically two or three at a time. After a decade of birthdays between the five of us, we had nearly 100. Additionally, the relative success of my small business had provided some financial flexibility and rather than stockpile cash in a bank, I purchased a small collection of gold coins as an asset that would be universally accepted in any kind of fallout.

Columbia Coin on Portland's east side was my stomping ground for purchasing coins and the owner, John Lock, is an amazing testament to old school business principles and family values. Every time I visit him I am invited back behind the display cases to his desk for a conversation that always centers around the recent happenings on all levels of our collective families as well as the relative state of our nation.

My visit in March of 2019 was no different. John and I sat down again and talked family life. But as you are now well aware, this visit was to sell our assets, not acquire more and our family had been through some significant turmoil. I shared all about the dreams, the accident, the words of counsel we received from the Lord, as well as the chaos that ensued leading up to the mediation.

As a side note, John is intentional with his attentiveness. When seated in conversation with him I am the only person in the room. Meanwhile, during our conversation his family greeted the other patrons and helped them with their requests, which made what happened next so surprising. It took about 15 minutes to relay to John all that had happened in our previous year and as usual he was intensely engaged with the conversation. I shared with him our perspective shift and about the offering we would make to the Lord. I told him about the settlement and how it felt like God was stretching us beyond what we thought we had.

With that, John abruptly stood and walked past me. It was as disruptive as it was abrasive and completely out of character. By the time I understood what he was doing he was nearly completed with his task and I didn't have the time to even begin to stand and join him.

This story gets better but for you to understand the impact it had on me, I need to remind you of the dream I had about my spinal cancer. The one that was incurable but would be treated by inserting a small piece of metal between discs seven and eight. Again, the question I posed the following morning had been:

God, why are you showing me this!?

Fast forward to now, at a time when I can look back with hindsight. This dream along with the others, especially the exorcism dream, was a prophetic dream from the Lord.

In wanting to better understand it, I found a website called CrossExamined.org that reposted a blog written by Brian Chilton. Brian has a M.Div. in Theology from Liberty University and a B.S. in Religious Studies and Philosophy from Gardner Web. He has received a certification in Christian Apologetics from Biola University and at the time of the writing was a student in the Ph.D. program in Theology and Apologetics at Liberty University. That's a long way of saying the dude has studied a thing or two about the Bible.

At any rate, in this blog post (https://crossexamined.org/reference-guide-biblical-numerology/) Brian discussed Christian Numerology and I specifically wanted to know what the numbers seven and eight meant.

According to the post, seven "is one of the most important numbers in the Bible. It symbolizes completion, perfection, and rest." The number eight "symbolizes new life, resurrection, a new covenant, and new beginnings."

So in my dream, I had a cancer in my spine between the discs that, according to this post, represented completion/perfection/rest and new life/resurrection/new covenant/new beginnings. I swear I'm not creative enough to make this stuff up.

AND... as if that wasn't enough, the only way to treat it was to insert a small metal disc directly into the cancer.

OK - Back to the story in the coin shop...

John had walked past me to his display case where he quickly pulled out his keys, unlocked the sliding door, grabbed a small container, locked the door and was on his way back to his desk.

Before he sat back down he stood in front of me, towering. It felt somewhat metaphoric, as if God was wanting to make something very clear.

Holding out the container he said, "This is not part of your estate. You cannot sell this. This is a gift."

I was a little taken aback, both by his abrupt interruption of the conversation as well as the insistence upon his offering. But I wasn't about to bring it up or argue with him... you don't look a gift horse in the mouth, right? (Google that one too if you don't follow.)

I took the container and began my assessment of a small coin, one that was significantly older than any coin I had ever held. It had the image of a scale stamped on one side and when I flipped it over there was an image of a small wheel on the other.

John sat down and proceeded to tell me that the coin was a Lepton, also known as a widows mite, and the significance of the gift immediately floored me.

Here was a coin, a small metal disc, that was being given to me as a gift after I shared the story of giving an offering of everything we owned. My cancer, as discussed earlier, was the love of money and in the dream the way to treat the cancer was with a small metal disc... just like the one John had given me representing our surrender of all of our money! (I SURE

HOPE YOU ARE SEEING THE CONNECTIONS HERE!)

The more I thought about all that God had been doing, the more I realized that this gift would be our standing stone, our Ebenezer.

"What's an Ebenezer?" you may be asking. No, it's not the character called Scrooge in the popular Christmas story. Be patient... I'll explain the Ebenezer later in this chapter.

I imagine that Jesus had sat waiting in the temple area for a while that day. He had his eyes fixed on the area near the depository for the temple treasury. He didn't need to sit next to it... the box was prominently placed in an area where men of high standing could be seen by all, placing their temple offering into its coffers. Finally, late in the day, the woman on whom Jesus had been waiting arrived and tentatively walked up the steps to the box. The men standing near it, acknowledging and accepting donations, payed her no heed as she added two small copper coins to its contents.

If they had noticed her, I'm sure they would have smiled and politely signaled her to step aside as another patron in a more ornate, more dignified robe approached. But it wasn't necessary, they paid her no heed. She stepped down and walked slowly toward the main temple gate, stopping only to look back through the great gate toward the inner sanctuary and the most holy place. I'd like to imagine that she saw Jesus at that point, smiled weakly, and walked out of the temple.

But the deed was not to be noticed, not to be seen. She had no desire for the attention of anyone in the area and those men certainly weren't going to acknowledge such a pitiful gift of a low standing woman. But Jesus took notice. Jesus saw her.

That afternoon as she arrived, Jesus interrupted the conversations going on around him and pointed her out to his guys. "Hey, see her? Watch this for a minute." Maybe he had already spoken with her, knew her story, knew her circumstance. (How else would the apostles have known she was a widow?) More than likely, she didn't have any family her husband was gone. If Jesus had in fact spoken with her, I wonder what he could have said to assure her that God would provide in her time of need.

Maybe she was past desperate… the two coins wouldn't have bought her an ounce of oil, let alone a loaf of bread; so what good would come from holding on to them? Or maybe she was just that faithful. Either way, how in the world was she able to give everything on which she had to live? Obviously, I've taken some liberty with the context of this story, but the book does say that Jesus points her out as being the righteous one among many who gave out of their wealth.

Now it would be a ridiculous overstatement to say that our life (Lauren and my own) resembled the widow's circumstance. We still had our careers, our family, our health and our home. But as I think back to that time in that coin shop, it seemed as if God was letting us know that he had taken notice. As he had with the widow, Jesus had seen our faith and he was providing yet another confirmation of his approval, something tangible that would serve as a reminder.

There's a popular hymn written in the mid-18th century titled "Come Thou Fount of Every Blessing." Cultural influences have shifted the dynamic of music played in today's churches, but the poetry within the lyrics of this hymn are astounding:

Come thou fount of every blessing, Tune my heart to sing thy grace.
Streams of mercy never ceasing, Call for songs of loudest praise.
Teach me some melodious sonnet, Sung by flaming tongues above.
Praise the mount, I'm fixed upon it, Mount of thy redeeming love.

Here I raise my Ebenezer, Here there by Thy great help I've come.
And I hope, by thy good pleasure, Safely to arrive at home.
Jesus sought me when a stranger, Wandering from the fold of God
He, to rescue me from danger, Interposed His precious blood.

Oh that day when freed from sinning, I shall see thy lovely face.

Clothed then in the blood washed linen, How I'll sing thy wondrous grace.
Come, my Lord, no longer tarry, Take my ransomed soul away.
Send thine angels now to carry, Me to realms of endless day.

Oh, to grace how great a debtor, Daily I'm constrained to be.
Let that goodness like a fetter Bind my wandering heart to thee.
Prone to wander, Lord, I feel it, Prone to leave the God I love.
Here's my heart Lord, oh, take and seal it, Seal it for thy courts above.

It's a powerful poem and song! I would encourage you to read it again if it hasn't fully sunk in. I personally have always wondered about the second verse of this song though, particularly the first line of the verse. "Here I raise my Ebenezer, Here there by Thy great help I've come." The following lines are relatively simple to decipher but I always glossed over line one figuring it may just be some 1750's slang, lost in translation.

Nope.

In 1 Samuel Ebenezer is referenced three different times. The first two mention it as a location where the Israelites camped prior to battle with the Philistines. In that battle, the Philistines overwhelmed the Israelite military and slaughtered over 30,000 soldiers. This all came about because Israel had chosen to walk away from the Lord and turned to worshiping idols… and not just bowing down to a piece of wood or stone. I'm talking about some of the craziest, horrific, and most despicable acts you can imagine. God was fed up with their behavior and he used the Philistines as a tool to rebuke his people. To add insult, the Philistines carried off the Ark of the Covenant after the battle leaving Israel in a physically, emotionally, and spiritually weakened state.

Eventually though, the Philistines realized they had made a mistake and returned the Ark to Israel. (Apparently when dealing with the Lord, taking a sacred object from its home leads to tumors, death, and a rat infestation!)

In the ensuing 20 years, the people of God repent of their idol worship and return to worshiping him. Somewhere around this time, the Philistines attack again and Samuel, in defense against an oncoming assault, leads Israel to a rout of the Philistine army. "Then Samuel took a stone and set it up between Mizpah and Shen. He named it Ebenezer, saying 'Thus far the Lord helped us.'" (1 Samuel 7:12)

The stone raised by Samuel after his victory over the Philistines is the Ebenezer. The name Ebenezer literally means "Stone of Help" and the symbolic gesture would remind the people that it was God alone who helped them overcome their enemy. The song references the stone saying, "… here there by Thy great help I've come." Meaning, "I've gotten here only by your great help Lord."

There's another instance of the Israelites raising a stone (or 12) to declare God's power. In the book of Joshua, God's people walk across the Jordan river on dry ground. Before proceeding across, Joshua tells one representative from each of the 12 tribes to pick up a large stone from the middle of the Jordan river and carry it to the other side.

> "On the tenth day of the first month the people went up from the Jordan and camped at Gilgal on the eastern border of Jericho. And Joshua set up at Gilgal the twelve stones they had taken out of the Jordan. He said to the Israelites, 'In the future when your descendants ask their fathers, 'What do these stones mean?' Tell them, 'Israel crossed the Jordan on dry ground.' For the Lord your God dried up the Jordan before you until you had crossed over. The Lord your God did to the Jordan just what he had done to the Red Sea when he dried it up before us until we had crossed over. He did this so that all the people of the earth might know that the hand of the Lord is powerful and so that you might always fear the Lord your God." (Joshua 4: 19-24)

God held back the waters and Joshua had 12 representatives grab large stones from the middle of the river and set them up once they crossed. The strange assortment of rocks was erected with no inscription or explanation, placed there so that future generations would be taught of the miracle: "God's power held back the waters for the good of His people… so remember to fear the Lord."

SO COOL! That's an Ebenezer! It's a reminder to God's people of his goodness and faithfulness. Joshua and Samuel set up stones. Moses sang a song when God delivered Israel from Egypt. New believers get baptized into the name of Jesus.

Our standing stone for this season would be a 2000-year-old coin, a widow's mite. It represented the cure to my spiritual cancer as well as the summary of work that God did in this season of our lives. It would serve as a reminder to us and to our children that God is faithful; that we could trust him, especially when going through difficulty. Holy Spirit had spoken to us on multiple occasions, guiding our approach and our obedience resulted in an overwhelming feeling of peace and submission to our refinement process.

Do you have a standing stone? An Ebenezer? What do you look to as a reminder of his goodness?

I've found that if we do not have a tangible Ebenezer, something to remind us of his goodness in times of difficulty, we will walk before he says "move", in a direction he did not point out, down a trail he did not clear, to a destination not of his choosing.

Our own sense of timing, direction and decision making are flawed. We screw things up. **Period.** It's just the nature of sin. If you need support for this point, read through the first few pages of the Book (Bible).

In the future, I will pull out that coin and remember this time. I'll remember his faithfulness. I'll remember the implications of the gift. And I'll teach my children of his goodness. We gave everything we could possibly give. It was the cure to my cancer and we had been given a confirmation that it was exactly what he had planned for us.

When we first moved to the cottage, I desperately wanted out but I look back now and I'm so grateful for the "hardship" it presented. My love of money, my cancer, my idol, was killing the Holy Spirit life within me. Then my golf dream showed how painful it was for God to know he was being replaced. But despite that, he pursued us and revived our hearts and has now taken us to a deeper level of intimacy with him.

He had and still has plans for my life but I needed major spiritual surgery before Holy Spirit could effectively work. Thank you Jesus for pressing pause on my ambition! Thank you God for your relentless pursuit! Thank you Holy Spirit for disregarding my restraining order!

God is SO good.

SO ASK YOUR QUESTIONS!

"REVIVE US LORD"

14

CHAPTER 14 — "REVIVE US LORD"

I used to think that my testimony was weak. I came from a believing household and heeded my parents advice when we had the uncomfortable discussions about drugs, alcohol or sex. Becoming a Christian was the easy part and it saved me from making a ton of stupid decisions. The funny part is that despite the influence of walking with Jesus, I still made a ton of stupid decisions!

Staying faithful is where things got difficult. God's perfecting process can be challenging, but the process is always intended to bring you to a new level, a new perspective, and with it a new authority.

This chapter is all about revival… something that I once thought was intended for non-believers. But the reality is I was unaware of my own need for revival. I was dry. Holy Spirit was voodoo, healings were fake, raising your hands in worship was 'religious', and Christian music was shallow. And yet I longed to see the power of God in my life. My guess is that some (not all) of you find yourself in the exact same place.

The revival of your heart, mind, and soul is not a direct result of your working for it… you can't control the process.

Read that again.

If anything, the opposite is true. A revived person was once dead (or at best lukewarm in the faith) and then something radical happens. In Ezekiel, God shows the prophet a vision of a valley filled with dried out human corpses. He then commands Ezekiel to proclaim a massive resurrection of Israel's army:

> Then he said to me, "Prophesy to these bones and say to them, 'Dry bones, hear the word of the lord! This is what the Sovereign Lord says to these bones: I will make breath enter you, and you will come to life.

> I will attach tendons to you and make flesh come upon you and cover you with skin; I will put breath in you and you will come to life. Then you will know that I am the Lord. (Ezekiel 37: 4-6)

God then commands Ezekiel to prophesy to the breath from the four winds and command the wind to enter the lifeless bodies and breathe new life into them. After the breath enters the "vast army" standing before him, God declares:

> Son of man, these bones are the people of Israel. They say, 'Our bones are dried up and our hope is gone; we are cut off.' Therefore prophesy and say to them: 'This is what the Sovereign Lord says: My people, I am going to open your graves and bring you up from them; I will bring you back to the land of Israel. Then you, my people, will know that I am the Lord, when I open your graves and bring you up from them. **I will put my spirit in you and you will live,** and I will settle you in your own land. Then you will know that I the Lord have spoken and I have done it, declares the Lord. (Ezekiel 37: 11-14)

Try to avoid the notion of zombies when God references opening the graves. This is a massive revival! God is actually having the prophet speak hope and life into the spiritually dead and lifeless people of Israel who had turned away from him to pursue foreign gods. That sounds oddly familiar to our culture!

While commonplace among the people groups surrounding the Israelites at the time, God's people would eventually come to observe unspeakable evils — participating publicly in sexual exploits in temples, even burning children in fire - both as acts of worship to false Gods. As a result, God uses the military might of the Assyrians and Babylonians to humble his people. Suffering defeat after each invasion, they would be displaced as slaves and bondservants in foreign lands, a people who had forfeited their homeland.

This scenario may sound foreign to us in the 21st century with our pocket-sized supercomputers and our interdependent global economy... There's no way we would ever participate in such barbarous and heinous acts. We're far too intelligent! Far too sophisticated! And we're so connected that war could not possibly break out! Right?

But here's where things get interesting... In the US, we are entrenched in a culture that has slowly allowed our calendars to be overrun by chaos. Bit by bit, time with the Father gets replaced by the demands of the schedule until spending dedicated time with Him becomes an inconvenience. The distractions of entertainment, wealth, sporting events, daily commutes, meetings, relationships, you fill in the blanks here... these all demand attention and we eventually run short on that currency.

And while our culture may be advanced, we're certainly not above the heinous atrocities exhibited by the people of Israel. Perhaps the only difference is that we perform these acts privately, out of view from the public eye. We won't ceremoniously sacrifice a child in the fire to a faceless god (Molek), but we certainly will sacrifice one for the sake of convenience (Hello Pro-Choice). And we won't go visit a shrine prostitute, but we'll certainly spend some time on that adult website. So are we really that different?

I don't write these words to shame or condemn, only to highlight the similarities between ancient Israel and us today. Another key similarity is that the Lord loves us as intensely today as he did Israel back then. And just like the valley of dry bones, He wants to revive us and breathe life into us, His army.

As a part of His army, the Lord does NOT want you merely outlasting the enemy. He wants you conquering and taking back ground. In his letter to the church in Corinth, Paul provides a word of encouragement to the church as he challenges them to use this life as a training ground for the next:

> Do you not know that in a race all the runners run, but only one gets the prize? **Run in such a way as to get the prize!** Everyone who competes in the games goes into strict training. They do it to get a crown that will not last, **but we do it to get a crown that will last forever!**
> (1 Corinthians 9: 24-25 - Emphasis added)

God wants you to run in the authority granted to you as His son or daughter, boldly living out his calling on your life and completing your time on earth having finished the race as one who trained to win! We already know that God is going to win the war (see Revelation for those details), but until that time, **he wants us winning our current battles as well!** Early in the letter to the church in Corinth, Paul instructs the believers to build wisely on the foundation he laid as he shared the gospel with them:

> If anyone builds on this foundation using gold, silver, costly stones, wood, hay or straw, their work will be shown for what it is, because the Day will bring it to light. It will be revealed with fire, and the fire will test the quality of each person's work. If what has been built survives, the builder will receive a reward. If it is burned up, the builder will suffer loss but yet will be saved — even though only as one escaping through the flames. (1 Corinthians 3: 12-15)

Paul's urging in this passage reflects the heart of the Father... a desire for you to build your life with durable materials that will be refined by and survive the "fire" of our life and its challenges, as well as our death.

But a sick person can't (and really shouldn't) train for a race. A dead person can't build a house. Before they dive into that work (the work to which God is calling them) they have to be revived!

We have to be revived!

So re-read the first highlighted section of this chapter.

It's true. We can't control it. We can't make it happen. So if that's the case, how then does revival come about? This is especially important to understand if we know we want it! And that desire will kick off the first component of revival. But before we get to that you need to understand this analogy: When you want to clean your house (I mean really do some deep cleaning) the mess is going to get worse before it gets better.

To deep clean your house, you have to move the couches and the beds away from the walls in order to expose all the little dust bunnies and hidden treasures before they can be vacuumed and wiped up. Your closets and kitchen cabinets need to be emptied before they can be wiped down and reorganized.

So before you even start the deep cleaning process, your house must become a complete disaster! Couches and beds will be out of place, your clothing will be laid out all over the bedroom, and plates, silverware, and pantry items will be all over the countertops. (And don't even get me started on the funk in the bathroom or the kids bedrooms!) In fact, for your home to be cleaned, the status of cleanliness and order must get worse before it gets better.

The same is true of revival! Life may get a little more chaotic, a little more messy, a little more (insert your desired adjective here) before it gets better... before you can see the effects of the revival God is bringing, before Jesus' love is fully felt, before Holy Spirit pours out his power in and through you.

Lauren and I experienced an absence of Holy Spirit's power when our lives were not aligned with his plan. Then, after he marched through our restraining order and we finally realized we wanted Him there, life got significantly more messy as he prepared things for cleaning.

Please hear me and consider our story when I say this: The mess is worth it! The end justifies the means and his ways are SO MUCH higher than ours! So let's kick this off... How do we jump-start a revival of our heart, mind and soul?

As I dove into the scriptures during the chaos of our life experience over the last two years, a few things began to jump out at me.

1. Admission

> If my people who are called by my name humble themselves, and pray and seek my face and turn from their wicked ways, then I will hear from heaven and forgive their sin and heal their land. (2 Chronicles 7:14)

Despite our inability to see all the spiritual activity going on around us, preparation for your arrival began long before you ever showed up to the revival party. But the party, the actual revival, kicks off with an admission of need. If you want a revival of your heart, mind, and soul, you'll need to ask for it! And God is waiting for this moment... it's a catalyst! A turning point. As mentioned, Holy Spirit positions our steps through life events to get you to this point of surrender and it's from this point that God begins the revival process. Often times, the biggest challenge you'll face leading up to this decision is overcoming the mental objections posed by the enemy. But don't go halfway as you admit your need for revival and don't get cold feet when you start to feel the ground shake in your world — you're getting close. **Revival will rock you!**

Honestly though, would you want it any other way? If you had the chance to drink from life-giving water and never thirst again, or eat from the tree of everlasting life, would you be satisfied with just one sip or a little nibble? No way man! I'm drinking that glorious liquid or stuffing my face with that delectable fruit until I can't handle any more! God pour out all your love or don't give me any! Don't tease me with just a sample God... I don't want the cruising Costco lunch version of your love! I want the real deal — I want it all!

If you're craving revival, the most important step to take is to acknowledge how badly you want and need it. Here's an example of that truth playing out. I have family involved with Alcoholics Anonymous and on a few occasions I've joined them at meetings. Before anyone dives into their testimony about a battle with alcohol, they always stand up and introduce themselves by saying their name and their addiction. "Hi, my name's Matthew and I'm an alcoholic." Then everyone else says "Hi Matthew" in response. At first, I thought this was a bit ridiculous. But as people shared their stories, I began to realize the power each person experienced in acknowledging their position before they began their struggle. In other words, each person had to admit that he/she was an alcoholic before they were really ready to do the work to get sober.

Now, in regard to AA, I fundamentally disagree that once an alcoholic always an alcoholic. It assumes one can never be cured or healed of this disease which directly contradicts the word of our God and the power within his miracles (and let's not get caught up on the details of alcoholism and an individual's genetic predisposition towards excessive alcohol consumption). My point is you can see that the true power behind the miraculous change begins with each person's admission of his or her position.

Those in AA acknowledge their disease. If you want revival, the process starts by acknowledging that a part (or all) of you is spiritually dead, sick or dying. Your flesh may not want to admit to its weakness, but God isn't going to force you into this process. You need to come to it on your own.

Interestingly, admitting your need for revival is not too dissimilar to your own original conversion experience. As soon as you recognized the effects of your sin, you found a need for a savior. The more you walked with him in obedience, the more life changed, your position changed and he continued the process of perfecting you that began at your moment of surrender.

But without the admission of our weakened state, our pride, self will, and/or ego will shut down any work that Holy Spirit wants to do on our character. Case in point, nothing changed in my walk with him until the realization that my walk was lacking... that I had cancer, that I was "a scared little boy afraid to trust his father." In each of those realizations, I discovered I was desperate for revival.

And here's the interesting part, we were still unaware of our need for revival even when Holy Spirit was positioning some of our life circumstances. But once our desire for something deeper became apparent, we cautiously waded into the reviving waters of his love... then, once we realized how good it was and is, we dove in headfirst.

If you want revival, you have nothing to lose by admitting your need. Jesus said, "What good is it for a man to gain the whole world and yet lose his soul?" (Mark 8:36)

Cry out to God. Ask Holy Spirit to prepare your path to begin the revival process and watch how your admission allows Him to begin coordinating circumstances in your life. He may, in fact, have already begun that process.

2. Position

> For this is what the high and exalted One says — he who lives forever, whose name is holy: 'I live in a high and holy place, but also with the one who is contrite and lowly in spirit, to revive the spirit of the lowly and to revive the heart of the contrite.' (Isaiah 57: 9)

Before we fully dove in, I didn't think I was spiritually sick or in need of a revival. We were leading a house church, my buddy got baptized in our creek, my wife and I were growing in our understanding of the word, we were giving to people in need, and God was leading us to minister in schools and in prisons. But as our setting shifted into a new home, a new church body, and a new season of life, we noticed something different about the people surrounding us. They spoke of an intimacy with the Lord that seemed to reach deeper. My pride prevented me from asking about it, but I felt a longing for that kind of connection with the Lord.

Can you relate with this? Do you get the sense that there could be a deeper level of intimacy with the Father? There is of course... We will forever be going deeper! And I believe God is constantly inviting us to go deeper.

But if we want to meet him there, in that deep and secret place, we need to be positioned differently than we have been in the past. This is the second key to revival. God is looking to partner with us. The prophetic word won't come to life unless you partner with it and do the prophetic work!

When my wife saved the man in the restaurant, she had to perform CPR to resuscitate him. But she faced a problem as she went to intervene: the man, who would have weighed in at over 300 lbs, laid crumpled on his side in his booth, surrounded by tables, chairs, and people. There was no room to maneuver. Everyone and everything surrounding him froze the moment he collapsed. As soon as she realized the need, Lauren shouted at people to get out of the way, move the chairs, move the tables. She yelled at a server (a big guy) to pull the unconscious, 300 lb. man out of the booth. Before she could begin the process of resuscitation, Lauren had to clear the area and move him into position… He had to be repositioned in order to be saved. We too must be repositioned for our own revival.

God moved us away from the farm, away from our familiar church setting, and into a very challenging season in the process of our revival.

This repositioning is a dance for two with a couple of intricate steps in the process. Holy Spirit arranges life circumstances on a macro scale while we go about arranging them on a micro-scale. But positioning is more than a change in circumstance. It's a change in behaviors that bring about a new mindset.

Before the repositioning for revival begins, it helps to understand that God is already pursuing you; that the Holy Spirit has been actively involved in your circumstances in an effort to bring you to a place where you're receptive to God's reviving power.

> "From one man He made every nation of men that they should inhabit the whole earth; and he determined the times set for them and the exact places where they should live. God did this so that men might seek after him and perhaps reach out for him and find him, though he is not far from any of us." (Acts 17: 26-27)

Knowing this should allow you to scoff at any hardship you face — but I know that's much easier said than done. Being secure in the sovereignty (knowing he's in control) will keep your blood pressure low and your stress levels manageable and will also allow you to walk with grace through the flames.

Once you're secure in God's love and pursuit of you, ask Holy Spirit to intervene in the chaos of life and position you for revival. It's that simple. Repeat aloud what you read next if you really want that deeper level of intimacy: "God I want revival. I need revival. I crave a deeper level of intimacy with you, Jesus. Please position me so you can pour out your healing power in my life."

It's really that simple. God lives in a high and holy place to revive the spirit of the lowly and revive the heart of the contrite." (See Isaiah 57:15 for God's declaration to this point.)

Ask God for help in arranging things for your revival and watch how he works. Then, begin to make changes in your daily habits so that you create space for the Lord to minister to your heart. This is what was meant by the prophetic work I mentioned earlier — Read the word, meditate on it, pray, listen and commune with Holy Spirit, throw on a worship playlist. These are just some practicals to pursue the Lord and listen for his voice. As this practice becomes a habit, your intimacy and connection with him will grow to the deeper levels you crave.

3. Release

> Create in me a pure heart, O God, and renew a steadfast spirit within me. Do not cast me from your presence or take your Holy Spirit from me. Restore to me the joy of your salvation and grant me a willing spirit, to sustain me. (Psalm 51: 10-12)

This is perhaps the most challenging step in preparing for revival.

> "Whoever wants to be my disciple must deny themselves and take up their cross and follow me. For whoever wants to save their life will lose it, but whoever loses their life for me and the for the gospel will save it." (Mark 8: 34-35)

Jesus' words pertain to control. In this life we can choose between one master or another but the option of not having a master is not a reality. We're either slaves to our sin or we're slaves to Jesus, and the most challenging part of being a voluntary, obedient slave to Jesus is releasing control of our own life.

As followers of Jesus, we are called to do as our master instructs. If we're summoned, we go. If we're sent out, we go. As we are given marching orders by Holy Spirit, we fulfill them out of love and obedience.

Now, we could get legalistic about Jesus' commands and follow His rules rather than His love. But if we did that, we'd miss the entire point of the cross. In Matthew 11 Jesus says, "Come to me all you who are weary and burdened, and I will give you rest. Take my yoke upon you and learn from me, for I am gentle and humble in heart, and you will find rest for your souls. For my yoke is easy and my burden is light."

Taking on the yoke of Jesus is just another way of saying we submit to his Lordship. And why wouldn't we want that? The son of God, the author of the universe is telling us it's the easier path, the one with a lighter burden. It's not just stepping into a life of chastity. It's realizing that the life God has planned out for us is infinitely better than any plan we could have concocted. And let's face it, if we were so good at planning and executing the strategy for our own lives, why would we find ourselves in need of a savior? Or a revival?

As your revival process begins, you will have a choice to make: Will you relinquish control and allow the Holy Spirit to work or will you rebel against the Lordship of Jesus? It's really that simple, albeit incredibly difficult to execute!

The song Fall Afresh has an incredible lyric that pertains to this kind of release of control and submission: "Spirit of the living God, come fall afresh on me. Come wake me from my sleep. Blow through the caverns of my soul, pour in me to overflow."

That kind of intimacy takes surrender! Asking God to make his way through the caverns of your soul and fill them to overflowing... that's powerful! And the sooner you can relinquish control of the process, the sooner that overflowing power will produce a radical change.

4. Patience

Restore us again, O God our savior, and put away your displeasure towards us. Will you be angry with us forever? Will you prolong your anger through all generations? Will you not revive us again that your people may rejoice in you? Show us your unfailing love, O Lord, and grant us your salvation. (Psalm 85: 4-7)

Now, that last sentence of section three would give the impression that revival can come as fast as you're willing to relinquish control... and if you think God is going to (and should) show up as soon as you give up that control, then you'd be inadvertently attempting to control the timeline of your revival process. Did you follow that? When you give up control of the process, you need to give up control of the timeline as well. In other words, be patient.

When you give up control of the process, you need to give up control of the timeline as well. In other words, be patient.

We had to endure three years of challenge in our most recent revival process and I'm not convinced we're completely done with this season of revival. There is still a tremendous amount of closure needed in order to see the big picture of how he has worked things out completely. Meanwhile, our family of five continues to live in our cottage... again, a two bedroom, one bathroom home. We know it's not a long term solution and we've shared with Him our frustration and concern about this setup. But we're surrendered to the process and we're patiently waiting on Him to make it clear where we should be going next and what we should be doing when we get there.

The really cool part is that we're getting close, we can feel it. Friends have mentioned they feel the Lord is about to impart a tremendous amount of clarity and understanding to us. We've also heard that He'll be pouring out abundant blessings on our family and all we need to do is say 'Thank you'.

Looking at new homes on Zillow can be a fun way to waste 30 minutes. Fantasizing about our family in a bigger home, in a new location, and back on property — it's exciting. At least it used to be. Then I realized that in playing the Zillow game, I was getting the cart ahead of the horse. God hadn't said, "It's time to go." So why was I toying with it? Why was I desiring a move after surrendering control of the process?

No one ever said being patient was easy. In fact it's the second hardest part of allowing God to revive your heart and soul. The process takes time. But the closer you get to it, the more momentum you feel behind you! I'm now to the point that looking at homes on Zillow is actually distasteful because I'm so confident that God has something far better for us than I can even imagine! Why would I want to interrupt that now?

The revival process brings with it a lighter feel to life. Refreshing begins to describe it but does not fully do it justice. It's like diving into a clear mountain lake on a hot summer day. There's just a level of contentment that arises in that experience — It's amazing!

But once there, it's not over. Revival is a wash, rinse and repeat process of continual refinement that actually began when you first believed. Life includes many revival moments and each is a testament to the unbelievable love the Father has for his children. Our challenge is to make sure we stay close to Jesus through the ups and downs of life. He'll do the rest.

> **Revival is a wash, rinse and repeat process of continual refinement that actually began when you first believed.**

Our enemy desires to interrupt the revival process and will frequently plant thoughts in your mind to make you question the timeline, circumstance, or people around you. Don't let that derail the good work God is doing in you. Admit your need, allow yourself to be positioned, release control, and then be patient, all the while basking in the love of our perfect and all-powerful Father in heaven. Our God is the good shepherd; he'll leave the flock of 99 to seek out the one who is lost. Be at peace in that. Know that God is seeking you out, as he does with all his children. Ask for the revival. He's wanting to begin that process more than you know.

"A SLOW EXORCISM"

CHAPTER 15 — "A SLOW EXORCISM"

We had just written a check for $119,500. It was the largest transfer of wealth we had personally ever experienced. Soon thereafter, one of my biggest temptations was to consider what we could have done with that money... New home? Vacation home? New car(s)? Exotic vacations? In other words, my new temptation was to regret what had happened, and in so doing, to forget how the Lord had worked.

Now that we were through it all, my heart was at peace; so whenever those thoughts came I dismissed them quickly, knowing that God would be our provider. I wasn't perfect... there were times when regret would attempt to remind me of what we had "lost", but my heart had been changed and my eyes had been opened to the status of my cancer.

My desire was no longer for security and a comfortable living that money could provide. More than anything I wanted my children to know God's goodness, his unfailing love, and his relentless pursuit of our hearts. If I had to sacrifice wealth to enable that, then so be it. And even today, I still submit this prayer somewhat regularly.

As my thinking about money shifted due to the severity of the disease, the voice suggesting I should think about it got progressively quieter.

> For the love of money is a root of all kinds of evil. Some people, eager for money, have wandered from the faith and pierced themselves with many griefs. (1 Timothy 6: 10)

The cancer that had been growing ever so slowly in my heart for 35+ years had been given a heavy dose of spiritual chemo. God had been dealing with my circumstance in the natural to affect and revive me in the spirit. I was breathing anew all over again. The bedrock sin, the core issue of my river dream (that held the pillars of the dam in place) had cracked and was crumbling as Holy Spirit life began flowing. It was an exhilarating experience!

Pillar 1 - Discontentment: I began to appreciate our home, our cottage. We started hosting people every week for dinner and dabbled in a small group. We knew it wasn't going to be a long term solution for our growing family (our firstborn was nine and he was eventually going to begin smelling of puberty) but we fell in love with the dynamic in the tiny house. Easy to clean, great for family interaction, and even better as a training ground for developing patience.

Pillars 2 & 3 - Fear & Anxiety: My concerns about money completely disappeared... Ha! Not quite, but they certainly diminished. Maybe it's because we didn't have anymore. HA HA! But seriously, I began feeling liberated from the concerns about how God would provide. Lauren had a fabulous career going and my work remained consistently strong. We received prophetic words of exponential financial growth from people who had no idea of our chaotic experience and knew that whatever came, God was and would be our provider.

Pillar 4 - Expectations: The expectations I had placed on my life were also evaporating. I had always wanted to be a successful entrepreneur like my father and the desire to make a lot of money and enjoy a great lifestyle was a big draw AND for the first time in our lives, Lauren and I were in a position to get ahead in the rat race. But I also felt a very real conflict in a call to ministry. That dilemma was highlighted one Sunday morning when my father accompanied us to worship. We heard a lesson on the archer's paradox, where the arrow actually has to be pulled backwards in order to be released forward by the bow.

My dad pulled me aside after the service and told me I had a calling on my life - that I was supposed to be teaching people about Jesus and preaching about God's goodness. He said it was time to release that arrow. It was one of the most powerful, life giving moments I had ever experienced with my father.

It was then I realized that the expectations I thought he had for my life were imaginary. For some reason, that enabled me to release my own expectations and enjoy the life we were living.

Thinking back to my first dream, the exorcism dream, I believe the love of money correlated with the demon that needed to be kicked out of my life. In going through this season of life, it was losing strength as I gained momentum in faithfulness.

Now, it's one thing to say "God will provide" when prosperity abounds, and the bank account is full. But when desperation and fear have joined you as guests at the dinner table, that phrase takes on a more challenging connotation. I don't mean to say we had everything figured out... we didn't and still don't. But the less I trusted in our finances, the more our faith grew (and continues to grow) in the Lord.

And it gets better. I began to feel Holy Spirit flowing through me on a more regular basis. We received several prophetic words about our future and the roles into which God was calling us and some crazy things began occurring.

On a hot Saturday afternoon in August I took my kids on an errand to Home Depot to pick up some things for the house. It was a busy day and we were wanting to get in and out of the giant warehouse as quickly as possible. I spoke with someone at the customer service desk to get a location for the items we needed and we bee-lined it in the direction of the first piece of hardware on the list.

As we walked through the gray and orange aisles, we made a sharp left turn through the power tool section and came upon a man and his son who seemed to be having a rather difficult time. The boy sat in the child seat of the orange cart, screaming at the top of his lungs, all the while hitting his head with his hand as hard as a child could. The father, unable to console his son, could only rest his hand on the boy's head in an attempt to diminish the blows as the boy raged on. It was clear something was wrong and as we walked past I could tell it was something deeper than a tantrum.

Evaluating the disposition of the father during the boy's melt down, I realized this must have been a common occurrence and that the boy was deep into the autism spectrum. The father could only let it play out. My children stared in dismay and my heart felt weighed down in sadness and sympathy for their situation. I remember thinking specifically, "Aarrgghh, that just sucks!" And then Holy Spirit chimed in.

Pray for him.

"Uhhh, I don't know Lord, that guy didn't look like a believer... He had tats all over his arms and did not have the appearance of someone who had any faith." My excuses were lame.

A lesson I had recently heard boomed into my ears: "I'd rather be obedient and wrong, than disobedient and right." (Thank you Sam!)

Now when I first heard this statement, I thought it was stupid. Blind obedience was the kind of mindset on which despots thrived. And it makes more sense to be disobedient to the surrounding culture and stand righteous before the Lord, right?

All that is true and good. But apparently, that teaching was in reference to the calling of the Spirit. The full teaching is this: I'd rather be obedient to the call of the Lord/Holy Spirit and possibly misinterpret it than disobedient to the call and be right about it, or worse, never really know. In other words, when God puts something on your heart it's better to go with it than to ignore it. You may hear correctly, or you could be wrong, but in the process, you will learn to decipher between your mental voice and the Spirit. You'll also see powerful transformations as Holy Spirit moves.

Pray for him.

I was already into another aisle before I really began wrestling with the objections. I felt a twinge of guilt and shame. Here I was with two of my three perfectly healthy kids, passing by a young child who clearly needed help and God was calling me to pray for him. Crap! Who was I to refuse?

"God, if you really want me to pray for that kid, let me see him again in the store."

This Home Depot was a monster, so there was a good chance that we wouldn't bump into each other again. I wouldn't seek out the twosome, but I would respond as directed if our paths crossed again.

We grabbed the remaining items on our list and headed back to the checkout area. I asked my oldest to pick an aisle that would be the fastest but as we were about to pull into his lane of choice, I saw (and heard) the boy clear across the front of the warehouse. I pulled out of our line to the dismay of my son and we headed in the direction of the boy (and the noise).

Before we arrived, the yelling had subsided but I caught up with the duo as they were about to wrap up their shopping trip. Unsure of what to say, I just kind of jumped in...

"Hey man, my name is Matthew, and this might sound a little strange but as we walked passed you two earlier I heard the Holy Spirit tell me to pray for your son."

"Oh, he's not my son, but thank you." The man replied and he continued walking down the aisle.

"Ummm, hey, no, you don't understand." I said. "I'd like to pray for him now. Would you mind?" As soon as I said that, the boy, who hadn't looked anywhere near my direction started up into one of his fits. He was screaming and repeatedly hitting his head again.

"Sure man, whatever." The caretaker said.

"Can I put my hand on his knee?" I asked over the tumult.

"Uhh, yeah, that's fine." He replied as he slipped his grown hand between the boy's head and the tiny hand slapping it.

I put my hand on the boy's knee and began to pray. It went something like this... "Father we thank you for your patience, your power and your grace. In the name of Jesus, I ask for healing on this boy (I can't remember his name now). God, let your love fall on him and fill him with a miraculous peace. If there are any spirits or forces plaguing him, causing him to act out and hurt himself they have no place here. We take full authority over them, we bind them, and we cast them out in the name of Jesus."

The very moment I said 'Jesus' in closing the boy stopped hitting himself, he stopped screaming, he stopped fidgeting. The autistic boy looked up and stared at me with deep blue eyes through long, disheveled blond hair, mouth slightly open... quiet.

"Woah." The guardian looked from the boy to me and back at the boy. He couldn't believe what had just happened. I couldn't believe what had just happened: full self-harming meltdown to a peaceful state of wonder.

"Have a great day!" I abruptly said and I peaced-out faster than what was probably comfortable for the guy. I couldn't stay there! What if the melt down started up again? My prayer had activated something and if the kid started up again, the little faith that was blossoming would be crushed... I had to get out!

We picked the shortest line in the checkout area and I asked my kids what they just witnessed, processing through it myself. "Dad, you just prayed for that kid and he stopped screaming and hitting himself." My oldest replied.

The boy and his guardian passed us a few minutes later on their way to the checkout and things were still calm. (Apparently we had chosen the shortest but slowest line in the store.) Five minutes later we were nearly done checking out when I heard a sound from the boy at the far end of the check out section. I cringed and looked in their direction and he was still good, but his eyes caught my attention again. They were locked onto me from across the store. The boy had just experienced a radical peace from the Lord, but his unyielding eye contact is what I remember most clearly about that day.

People on the autism spectrum get uncomfortable making eye contact, but this kid was staring into my soul. He didn't say thank you but he didn't have to... something had him in bondage and torment and Holy Spirit released him from it. There was a gratitude on that kid's face, a peace that emanated from him and my hope was that the drastic changes witnessed in the boy would have a similar spiritual impact on the faith of his guardian.

I felt like I was coming back to life. The more I trusted the father and the less I focused on money, the more I felt a revival of my soul, a peace in my spirit and a supernatural power to take on the enemy.

There were so many questions that had been asked during the two year period of testing and God had patiently allowed me to ask them and complain through asking them again. But looking back I realized I was asking all those questions in fear as I clung to the side of a cliff.

Yes, a cliff, it's the best analogy I could think of as I'm telling you the story. I was clinging to the side of a cliff and as long as I held on, I was safe. The cliff was money and the higher I tried to climb, the more slippery the rocks became but going down wasn't an option. In fact, I couldn't even look down; I had come too far. The questions I most commonly posed during our ordeal were:

"God, what is going on!?" or "What are you doing!?"

"Why?" was also a pretty common one at the time.

I was exhausted from holding on to the cliff for so long but terrified about letting go and falling. But God wasn't going to let me fall. In fact, he wanted me to get some perspective on the situation and see that I was only a few inches off the ground... I just needed to let go and step off to rest and be at peace. "Hey bud, I got you!"

And then Lauren began to have dreams. Crazy dreams. Dreams that made me uncomfortable at first and even more so later on.

"I need a break from work." She told me one day in June of 2019. "No problem." I said. "Isn't your sabbatical coming up soon?"

"No, I want to resign." She said.

And then I jumped right back on the cliff and gripped it hard!

"Wait a second..."

I thought through some of our recently created financial goals. We had posted a savings thermometer on the refrigerator (like what the kids in elementary school do to show their progress during a fundraiser). We were game planning how to recover from the settlement and pay off our mortgage in a 2-year period. We wanted to buy another home in cash over the next 5-7 years. We were in a great position to do this! And hadn't the Lord placed us here?

"... why do you want to resign?" I incredulously asked.

Her response was very matter of fact. "I had a dream and I've been hearing some things from the Lord. I think he wants to meet me in a place of rest, and

I can't do that while I'm working."

Holy smokes! Holy Moses!

My wife has an incredible career going for her... just 9 months earlier she had been promoted to a Director within the finance division of her company and had outperformed everyone's expectations. Her boss raved about her performance and her compensation package was fantastic! Dreams were good for insight, and prophetic words were great bits of encouragement to propel us into our calling, but was God really calling my wife to step out of her career?

God, why are you asking her to do this now!?

Slowly, very slowly, and very deliberately, I released my death grip on the metaphoric wall and stepped off, releasing whatever imaginary control I thought I had.

If the Lord wanted to use my wife, then who was I too arrest her development? I was not going to allow that demonic force, the love of money, to replant a seed in my soul. The Lord would provide. I'd rather the two of us be obedient to the call and possibly be mistaken than be disobedient and uncertain. Father, do what you will.

141

"ONGOING CONFIDENCE"

CHAPTER 16 — "ONGOING CONFIDENCE"

For you to understand the complete release of control around my wife's resignation, I need to take you back to October of 2018. By this point, as I have previously mentioned, my overnight dreams had gone into hibernation and it seemed God was intent upon me focusing on the river, my river. My work during the day was consistently busy. I was running a real estate media business at the time and was just wrapping up the busiest season of the year. Despite the success that had come with the work, I always longed for more in my career; it too had been a consistent battle of contentment.

A friend of mine who runs a decent sized media company in Portland asked me to join his team as a department lead, a Director of Media Production for his growing list of global clientele. It was something we had discussed in the past and I was thrilled that I was being given a shot. It brought me one step closer to a transition that I had played out in my mind. One that took me out of the insecurity of solopreneurship, into a role where I could again work with a team to build something cool. I love building (and the game of capitalism) and I was excited about the opportunity!

But something in the back of my mind didn't sit right. Interestingly enough, that very night I had a dream that had incredible significance on our future and on Lauren's resignation.

My family and I had just stepped onto the local Portland metro (the MAX). Two of my three kids and Lauren had taken seats toward the front of the train while I stayed back to look out the windows (our third child was oddly not in the dream). We headed west out of Portland, through the tunnel and up the hill towards the Oregon Zoo.

As I looked out the window, a gang of dump trucks came racing up the hill weaving in and out of traffic and quickly passed our vantage point on their way out of the city. I was enamored with them. Each truck had a load of firewood in the truck bed. After a good number of them had passed our train, a semi-truck and trailer, filled with more firewood came up quickly behind them. Maybe the semi was a refueling truck and their firewood was the source of their boosting power? At any rate, I was completely enthralled with the scene.

Then suddenly the train began speeding up unnaturally fast. We quickly passed traffic and eventually gained on the trucks I had just seen. I knew I was on the train but my perspective was above it where I could see both the train and the highway. Once we passed the trucks, the train began bumping around on the tracks as it quickly approached a tunnel. I ducked into the train just as we entered and the windows went dark.

At this point, I started getting uncomfortable with the change in speed and turbulence so I made my way to the front car to check on Lauren and the kids.

When I arrived, the train was relatively empty and a woman I didn't recognize was sitting next to Lauren. The kids, my kids, were sitting nearby making a fuss and they either needed help or discipline. I couldn't tell which, I just knew in that moment they needed their mother and she wasn't responding. My attention quickly turned to Lauren.

She was out of it... eyes open but vacant. I reached out to touch her arm but she quickly pulled away on contact, like my fingers burned her skin. I felt frustrated that she had been so disengaged from our children but as I tried to speak with her about it, she slouched down in her seat and passed out.

Surprised, I looked at the woman next to her who became visibly uncomfortable with my presence. When it became clear she was about to change seats I demanded to know what had happened. Somehow I knew Lauren had been drugged and I knew this stranger had done it... and there was no way I was going to allow her to leave without an explanation.

After demanding an answer, she said she had taken out a syringe and that during the turbulence of the train speeding up she had bounced in her seat and brushed up against Lauren who had inadvertently received a full dose of some kind of sedative.

I knew it was a lie. I knew someone (some spiritual power) had targeted my wife in an attempt to subdue her. Whoever or whatever this power was, it didn't care to kill her. It simply wanted to disarm her, make her strategically inept, neutralize her.

I gathered Lauren in my arms and the other woman got up to leave. She walked away in tears having realized what she had done, the evil she had committed. Lauren was in my arms, heavily sedated and I knew she needed help.

The next thing I remember the two of us (her still in my arms) were at a beautiful farm where a bunch of people were working around raised garden beds on the top of a small hill. It was near dusk and the sun was casting a beautiful golden hue on everything and everyone on the farm. I knew a good friend of ours was there and I needed to get Lauren to her for help. After a brief search, I found her conversing with another woman I recognized. But it was weird, I knew the other woman was familiar but only by the feeling I got when I looked at her, not because I recognized her appearance. Then I woke up.

The odd part about the ending of this dream was that afterwards I realized the same woman that was with our friend had also been by my side while I was on the train. She was the one who had subtly let me know that Lauren needed help, that she had been drugged by the woman sitting next to her, that she needed rescuing. It hit me then that this woman was the Holy Spirit.

I poured over the dream the following morning and I came to the conclusion that the new work opportunity would be a distraction that would put my wife and family at risk. We weren't yet out of the woods with the accident, mediation, and settlement so a role that would require travel and further interruption of our daily schedule would be overwhelming to our family. I called my friend later that afternoon and turned down the offer.

After Lauren's promotion to Director of Finance, her responsibilities at the office increased. Where before she could leave to pick up the kids at four o'clock, she now had to stay at the office until five-thirty or six, sometimes even as late as seven in the evenings, particularly when the busy season was in full swing. It was a dramatic change for our family life but I did my best to support her in the transition.

As previously mentioned, Lauren performed fantastically in this new role, she was killing it. But over time it became clear that something was killing her. Her mental capacity was consumed with work. There was little to no downtime - not because the downtime didn't exist but because every available moment was consumed by work, thoughts of work, ideas about how to solve problems at work... it was never-ending. That fact, along with her condition in my dream, should have tipped me off to what was really going on.

Being an adult, I was able to fight for the time and attention of my wife. I need her in my life and I'm not afraid to address this need if/when we've been distant. But as an example, I would be in the middle of giving her a back massage before bed and would ask what she was thinking about and it always went back to work... even if ten seconds prior, we were talking about something else. She was distant and disengaged with me and I didn't like it.

The kids were less demanding because, as kids, they don't yet know how to fight for the time or the affections of their mom (short of crying or throwing a fit - but they're beyond that stage now). They felt her absence but didn't know how to express it. When I was not available for them, they were left on their own.

Interestingly enough, God never demanded Lauren's time or attention either. Holy Spirit never disrupted her phone calls or meetings at the office, nor did he interrupt her brainstorming in the evenings. But in her focus on the work, she became deaf to God's calling - exactly what the enemy wanted. Through the principality of busyness and the pursuit of career success, the enemy was having a field day in the process of sedating my wife to her calling. It took a few months for me to realize it but my initial assessment of the dream and its implications were wrong.

Lauren had already been attacked, sedated by the work in this new role. The job offer I had received and my distraction in the dream didn't lead to her sedation. If anything it allowed me to walk into the setting with an ability to see clearly that she had already been sedated. It was now my job to rescue her and take her to a place where she could recover.

And this brings us to the present day, early October of 2019. Lauren has announced her resignation, which will take effect at the end of this calendar year. She is halfway through a 6-week sabbatical that started in the middle of September and returns in early November to help transition a successful handoff of the role... And then she's done!

I'm going to do my best to support my wife as she resets, rests and experiences a season of revival with the Lord. I don't know what that's supposed to look like but I'm excited about the implications: My kids will get their mom back, I'll get my wife back and the Lord is going meet with her and pour into her the wisdom and power and love that will end up overflowing so she can pour it out to others.

My cancer is in remission but this calling is evidence to support the theory that God is working to further suppress the love of money within me. With this move, our Ebenezer had more than doubled in value. Lauren was walking away from a very beneficial compensation package and that coupled with the settlement offering made for a rather valuable reminder that money would not be my idol!

While my thoughts occasionally meander back to the financial implications of the change, we know that God is our provider. More recently I've been given images of the pillars of the dam falling over in disrepair as the underlying bedrock, (my love of money) continues crumbling. I'm still working on being diligent in my time with the Lord each day, but I feel renewed, refreshed. More than that I feel God leading me toward a designated purpose. Holy Spirit life is certainly flowing in my river and I am grateful he was persistent enough to walk through my restraining order to revive my heart and soul.

As I mentioned in the introduction of this book, there is a calling on your life. You have been created with a specific purpose in mind and God's kingdom is lacking until you step into it.

Ask your questions. He can take your skepticism and lack of faith. He's waiting with anticipation for you to pour out your heart so he can share his own with you. When that happens, your faith will grow in tremendous bounds.

What I haven't mentioned up to this point is that our story itself was a response to a question that I posed to the Lord.

In my youth I would quite often make requests of God (two in particular) that now give me pause. The first is a request for knowledge. I believe this question pleases the Lord and I believe he loves doling out that resource. But usually this comes in the form of discipline following a poor decision.

The second question is the one that I really have to stop and consider before asking. Knowing that hardship brings with it the fruit of growth and personal development, I asked God for a season of hardship before all this went down, and the Lord gave us EVERYTHING we could handle.

And I ask myself the same question you're probably asking... "Why in the world would I ever make such a dumb request!?"

I'm not a glutton for punishment or hardship. I believe we're all slowly growing into the calling God placed on our lives. But I like the outcome and development that follows a season of hardship. I think it puts us into a turbo growth mode (if you can imagine such a thing).

While I want to encourage you to consider making this request to the Lord, it would not be fair of me to challenge you with it without also providing the following disclaimer:

God will answer this one.

You will undoubtedly be given a green light for hardship stemming from your desire to grow. SO, don't be afraid of that question or the desire to grow into your calling; but if and when you ask for the hardship, brace yourself. He's not going to give you more than you can handle (1 Corinthians 10:13) but he will give you exactly what you need.

This is certainly not the end of our story, but it's the end of **this** story so I'll close, again sharing this passage from Psalm 27:

> **"I remain confident of this: I will see the goodness of the Lord in the land of the living. Wait for the Lord; be strong and take heart and wait for the Lord!"**